THE DEMENTIA CAREGIVING GUIDE

Empowering techniques to understand and manage symptoms with compassion, enhance quality of life, and maintaining your own well-being

Suniti Barua, PhD

Dedication

To my Guru Ji Swami Avdheshanand Giri Ji Maharaj and my Grandmother, whose continued blessings and unwavering belief in me have been my guiding light.

To my Dad, Mom and Badi mom, whose enduring love has been my strength.

To my Parents-in-Law, for their boundless wisdom and encouragement.

To my husband, my rock, thank you for your steadfast support and love.

To my siblings, my forever cheerleaders, thank you for always standing by me.

To my children, my endless inspiration, you give my life purpose and joy.

And to all the caregivers, you are heroes!

Acknowledgements

I extend my deepest gratitude to my editor, Karen Harris, for their insightful feedback and dedication; my formatter, Abdul Rehman, for ensuring the final product is impeccable; and my illustrator, Sawaroj Vashiraphiphob, for bringing the book's concepts to life through beautiful illustrations. This book is a testament to the collaborative effort of these talented individuals, and I am profoundly grateful for their contributions.

TABLE OF CONTENTS

INTRODUCTION

Love, strength, patience, courage, and an unyielding resilience. These are adjectives we often use to describe a loved one who is battling dementia, one of the cruelest, most heartbreaking of all diseases. These same adjectives can also be used to describe you, the caregiver of a loved one with dementia. If you find yourself reading this, it's likely you're familiar with the unique challenges of dementia care. You are not alone. According to a 2014 study, "Caregiver Burden: A Clinical Review," which appeared in *JAMA*, there are more than "43.5 million individuals providing support to midlife and older adults." This number is only growing year after year. Although you may often feel alone and isolated in your caregiving journey, millions share your experience.

Caregivers are the unsung heroes of those who suffer from dementia. They are responsible for much more than just basic care. They provide comfort, create a safe and understanding environment, and offer companionship through the ups and downs of the loss of memory and awareness. Caregivers – either family members or healthcare professionals – must navigate the complex requirements of dementia care while watching a person they love lose their independence and dignity. Despite the challenges, many of the caregivers I have encountered describe the caregiving process as transformative.

My journey into understanding the world of dementia caregiving began in the halls of nursing homes and skilled nursing facilities. In the capacity of a clinical psychologist, I had the privilege of working closely with the elderly and their families. It was there, amidst the daily triumphs and trials, that I witnessed the profound impact dementia has not only on those it directly afflicts but also on the loved ones tasked with their care. These experiences laid the foundation for this book, crafted with the hope of providing support and guidance for those navigating this challenging path.

This book's mission is clear: to empower you, the caregiver, with practical techniques and compassionate strategies that enhance symptom management and self-care practices. My goal is to improve the quality of life for both you and your loved one, providing relief and a sense of control in a situation that often feels anything but manageable.

What sets this guide apart is its focus on offering easily accessible, chapter-specific guidance, tailored specifically to the needs of adult children caring for parents with dementia or Alzheimer's. It has been designed to be a resource you can turn to time and again. It's a place where you can find relevant information quickly, whether you're facing a new symptom, a difficult decision, or just need a reminder that you are doing an incredible job.

The prevalence of dementia is staggering, with millions diagnosed worldwide. Countless families have been affected by its reach just as yours has been. In fact, families often rely on one or two of its members to step into caregiving roles when needed, as this is a more cost effective and caring solution. Based on the article "Dementia Care Spending by State: 2010–2019" published in the Journals of the Alzheimer's Association, informal dementia care led to a loss of $58 billion in wages in the United States in 2019. The cost of replacing informal dementia care with health aides would have been $230 billion. The expenses associated with dementia care vary significantly by state, even when calculated per prevalent case. It's anticipated that these costs will nearly double by the year 2050.

This book acknowledges the gravity of this issue, not with despair but with a determined optimism, highlighting the critical need for comprehensive, empathetic support for caregivers like you.

Within these pages, you'll find anecdotes from my professional experience and stories from fellow caregivers, offering real-world insights and practical advice that make this guide not just informative, but relatable and actionable. I understand the skepticism that can come with seeking out new resources, the doubt that perhaps there is nothing left to try. Let me assure you, this book offers fresh perspectives and innovative strategies grounded in the latest research and my extensive experience in the field.

I encourage you to engage actively with this book, applying its insights and strategies in your caregiving journey. Consider it a supportive tool and a companion in the complex world of dementia caregiving. This book is designed to navigate you through understanding dementia, practical caregiving strategies, legal and financial planning, and, importantly, caregiver self-care.

As we delve into this guide together, I want to conclude this introduction with a message of hope and empowerment. Understanding, compassion, and the right strategies can significantly improve your quality of life and that of your loved one. Through this book, I aim to light your path, offering a roadmap to a place where love, care, and knowledge intersect, empowering you to face the challenges of dementia caregiving with strength and grace.

To help guide and balance you during your caregiving journey, I want to gift you with affirmations at the end of the book.

Chapter 1

FACTS ABOUT DEMENTIA

Understanding the nuances of this terrible disease is the first step in establishing a compassionate care plan that will set you up for success in your new role as caregiver. The task of understanding dementia, therefore, becomes not just an academic endeavor but a deeply emotional journey into the heart of what it means to love, to lose, and to find strength in vulnerability.

1.1 By the Numbers

The Alzheimer's Association publishes an annual report to provide up-to-date facts and statistics about dementia and Alzheimer's disease to inform patients, families, caregivers, the government, and healthcare professionals about the prevalence of this disease. According to their 2024 report:

- Approximately 6.9 million Americans are living with dementia.
- Seventy-three percent of dementia patients are age 75 or older.

- Three out of every five dementia patients are women.
- More than 11 million Americans provide unpaid care for a family member or friend with dementia, a contribution to the nation valued at nearly $350 billion.
- Two-thirds of dementia caregivers are women.
- Fifty-nine percent of family caregivers of people with dementia rated the emotional stress of caregiving as high or very high.
- Eighty-three percent of the help provided to older adults in the United States comes from family members, friends or other unpaid caregivers.

1.2 Myths About Dementia

Dementia is often misunderstood, leading to myths and disinformation. One myth is that only the elderly are affected, but this is untrue. Younger people can also be diagnosed with forms of dementia, such as frontotemporal dementia, a disease that often impacts people in the prime of their lives. The mistaken belief that dementia is an "old person's disease" delays diagnoses and support for younger people.

Many people believe that dementia is an unavoidable part of getting older ... that it happens to everyone eventually. On the Alzheimer's Disease International online fact sheet, there is a bullet point stating, "Almost 62% of healthcare practitioners worldwide incorrectly think that dementia is part of normal aging". This idea neglects the fact that various diseases or injuries affecting the brain can result in dementia. Alzheimer's disease and strokes, for example, can damage the brain's pathways. Understanding this distinction is crucial, not only for comprehending dementia but also for cultivating a compassionate and knowledgeable approach to its management and care. It's important to recognize that dementia is not an inevitable side effect of aging, but rather the result of a specific condition or injury to the brain.

Another myth is that dementia is contagious. This is categorically false. Dementia is caused by a combination of genetics, environmental factors, and lifestyle influences, and cannot be spread through touch or proximity. This myth can cause isolation and fear, and prevent communities from providing support to those affected by the condition.

Yet another myth is that there is only one form of dementia – Alzheimer's disease. In reality, there are several kinds of dementia. Each form of this disease is unique, with different impacts on cognition, personality, and daily life. Alzheimer's, for example, affects memory, while frontotemporal dementia can cause sudden changes in behavior and language, and Lewy body dementia can cause fluctuating cognition. It's important to understand these differences in order to provide tailored care and support.

Stigma surrounding dementia is fueled by these myths, and can prevent people from seeking help or discussing the condition. Education and awareness campaigns are essential for dispelling these myths and promoting understanding and support. Public education initiatives, such as community seminars and national campaigns, can help to address the needs of individuals and families affected by dementia.

By challenging stigma, dispelling myths, and promoting understanding, we can alter public opinion about dementia and create a more compassionate and empathetic community for those affected by this disease.

1.3 The Brain and Dementia: A Layman's Guide to Neurology

Dementia disrupts the delicate balance of our thoughts, memories, and emotions by affecting the intricate network of neurons and synapses in our brain. This condition causes the loss of connections, neurons, and, ultimately, the essence of our being. Understanding which parts of the brain are most vulnerable to dementia is key to unraveling this relationship.

The cerebral cortex – the brain's outer layer, renowned for its role in memory, thought, and judgment – often bears the brunt of dementia's impact. Here, in the folds and grooves of the cortex, the loss of neurons translates into the memory lapses and poor judgment that herald the onset of the disease. Simultaneously, the hippocampus – found within the cortex and pivotal for forming new memories – is impacted by dementia's progression, rendering the ability to learn new information or recall recent events a formidable challenge.

Neurodegeneration, the underpinning of dementia's progression, entails more than the mere loss of neurons. It's a complex series of biological failures that lead to the symptoms witnessed in dementia. This process begins with the buildup of abnormal proteins. In diseases like Alzheimer's, these proteins form plaques and tangles that interfere with neuron function and communication. Neurons not only lose their ability to communicate, they wither and die, leading to the cognitive decline characteristic of dementia. The degenerative process of dementia can be halted or slowed if the disease is detected early and treatment is sought immediately.

It's important to note that we have the power to prevent and preserve brain health. The lifestyle choices we make throughout our lives can, and do, impact overall brain health, offering a tangible means of potentially delaying the onset of dementia symptoms. A diet rich in omega-3 fatty acids, antioxidants, and vitamins, combined with regular physical activity, has been shown to bolster brain function and protect against cognitive decline. Similarly, engaging in mentally stimulating activities, from puzzles and reading to learning new skills, nurtures a resilient brain, capable of forming new neural connections even in the face of aging. Social engagement, too, plays a crucial role, with strong social networks and meaningful relationships acting as a buffer against the isolating tide of dementia.

Genetics play a role in dementia, however we should look at it as a predisposition rather than destiny. While certain genes have been linked to an increased risk of developing types of dementia, including Alzheimer's, this genetic inheritance does not guarantee the disease's onset. Rather, genetics, combined with a multitude of environmental and lifestyle factors, contribute to an increased likelihood of a patient developing dementia.

Medical science is making great strides in the realm of dementia research. With new understandings of the brain's complexities, the potential for new treatment options increases. Scientists are delving deep into the molecular intricacies of the disease to study the root causes of protein buildup and neuron loss. Groundbreaking research into the role of the immune system in neurodegeneration offers a new avenue for potential therapies, suggesting that modulating the brain's immune response could alter the course of the disease. Meanwhile, advances in imaging technologies are providing unprecedented insights into the brain, allowing doctors to observe the earliest changes that signal the onset of dementia.

Current clinical trials are exploring a range of potential treatments, from drugs designed to clear abnormal protein accumulations to therapies aimed at protecting and repairing neuron function. While the quest for a cure continues, the focus on early detection and intervention holds the most promise for slowing disease progression and preserving quality of life for those affected by dementia.

As a caregiver navigating the complexities of dementia, understanding the mechanisms that underlie the disease is vital. Why is your loved one experiencing drastic mood swings? Why is he or she forgetting words in a conversation? Why doesn't this person remember his or her own children and grandchildren? Once you understand that the damage to their brain is what is causing your loved one to act differently, you can set aside your own frustration and address the situation with a mix of science and logic and love and empathy. Research into the causes and treatments of dementia is ongoing and scientists are committed to understanding and improving brain health, not only for those currently facing dementia but for future generations.

1.4 The Different Types of Dementia: From Alzheimer's to Lewy Body

Dementia can cause forgotten memories and altered personalities. Each type of dementia can feel like a different pathway, with its own set of unique characteristics. It is important to remember that different people may experience different symptoms as their dementia progresses. Understanding these variants is akin to deciphering a complex map of the human brain, where every turn represents a potential shift in cognition, behavior, and emotional well-being.

Alzheimer's Disease

The average person often links Alzheimer's disease and dementia together, however they are not interchangeable terms. Alzheimer's Disease, which affects millions of people, Is a form of dementia that gradually erodes memory and alters behavior. Amyloid plaques and tau tangles disrupt the brain's architecture, leading to neuronal death. Alzheimer's first manifests as minor forgetfulness and later evolves into profound disorientation and a loss of recognition of loved ones. It also causes behavior changes such as agitation, withdrawal, and shifts in personality. Caregivers must adapt to an ever-changing landscape of needs and emotions.

Vascular Dementia

Vascular dementia is a cognitive impairment caused by reduced blood supply to the brain. It follows small or significant strokes, leading to brain damage that affects confusion, disorientation, trouble speaking or understanding speech, confusion, numbing, difficulty walking, poor balance, numbness or paralysis, sudden or headache. Unlike Alzheimer's, vascular dementia may progress in a stepwise manner with periods of stability and noticeable declines. This condition highlights the important link between vascular health and cognitive functioning, such as planning and judgment, the ability to pay attention, social functioning, among others.

Lewy Body Dementia

Lewy body dementia (LBD) is a complex disorder that blurs the lines between cognitive disorders and physical ailments. It's characterized by abnormal protein deposits known as Lewy bodies within brain cells, which cause a range of cognitive, behavioral, and motor symptoms. People with LBD experience symptoms such as hallucinations, sleep disturbances, and cognitive fluctuations. Additionally, LBD shares similarities with Parkinson's disease dementia, as both conditions involve cognitive decline and physical symptoms like tremors and rigidity.

Frontotemporal Dementia

Frontotemporal dementia (FTD) affects the frontal and temporal lobes of the brain, which control behavior, personality, and language. Unlike other types of dementia, FTD often occurs in younger individuals and can cause a decline in social norms and inhibitions, apathy, inappropriate behavior, and language and communication problems. You might have seen it on the news that a well-known actor, Bruce Willis, has been diagnosed with this condition.

Caregivers and loved ones must understand the medical aspects as well as the emotional and behavioral shifts that come with each type of dementia. The map of dementia includes Alzheimer's, vascular dementia, Lewy body dementia, and frontotemporal dementia, and requires careful management and personalized care.

Chapter 2

GETTING A DEMENTIA DIAGNOSIS

Dementia is not a single disease, but rather a complex set of symptoms that affect memory, thinking, and social skills so much that it disrupts daily life. It's important to recognize that cognitive impairment is not a normal part of aging but rather a result of damage to brain cells and communication ability. When disruptions occur in the brain's network of connections and pathways, it results in symptoms that collectively define dementia.

2.1 Understanding the Basics of Dementia

As noted by the World Health Organization, "Dementia is currently the seventh leading cause of death and one of the major causes of disability and dependency among older people globally." Dementia can cause a range of different symptoms that can make it difficult for people to continue with their daily lives. These symptoms can be unsettling and require people to adapt to new routines. However, by recognizing the early signs of dementia, we can begin to provide the support and care that those affected need. This requires empathy, resilience and a commitment to navigate the complexities of dementia with dignity and care. By doing so, we can create an environment that supports those with dementia and helps them to maintain their respectability and quality of life.

2.2 Recognizing Early Signs and Symptoms

It's important to understand the critical role early detection plays in managing dementia. It can make all the difference in improving the quality of life for those affected by this condition. Early diagnosis offers individuals and their families a precious window of opportunity to seek treatments that might slow the progression of symptoms, to access support services, and to make legal and financial arrangements that reflect the wishes of the individual. Moreover, early detection opens the door to the possibility of participating in clinical trials, contributing to the advancement of research and the potential discovery of new treatments.

Dementia often begins with subtle signs that may not be immediately attributed to the disease. However, the earlier we can recognize these signs and symptoms, the better equipped we can be at providing timely support and intervention.

- Memory Loss - One early indicator is memory loss... not typical forgetfulness like forgetting where you put your keys, but the kind of memory loss that affects daily life. It involves forgetting the names of people you know well or the significance of important dates. Even struggling to remember information you recently learned could indicate the early stages of dementia.
- Lack of Problem-Solving Skills - In early dementia, the patient may experience new-found challenges in planning or solving problems, tasks that were once second nature to the person now present with great difficulties. Imagine being a lifelong cook, but now the measurements and recipes are hard to understand, making it difficult to prepare a meal.

- Confusing Time and Place - This is more than just feeling confused for a short time. It's a big problem understanding where and when things are happening. The seasons and dates might not make sense anymore. The person might forget how to get to the hardware store or a friend's house.
- Difficulty with Visual Images - The brain processes visual information differently, so things can seem foreign and unfamiliar. Depth perception can be off, spatial relationships are off, distances can look different, and colors may not be as bright. Reading can be difficult, and even stepping down a curb can be scary.

Dementia symptoms may be subtle at first, but they accumulate and worsen over time. It's important to pay attention to the nuances of our loved ones' experiences, even when it's difficult. We need to have conversations that can lead to better understanding and preparation.

The symptoms of dementia can be unsettling both for patients and caregivers. Just when you have one routine in place, you may have to adapt to a new one. However, by recognizing the early signs of dementia, we can jumpstart the care that those affected need.

2.3 Diagnosing Dementia

Diagnosing dementia starts with gathering a medical history, where healthcare professionals listen to patients' stories and piece together a preliminary picture of their cognitive health. Then, doctors conduct physical examinations, blood tests, and neurological evaluations to rule out other conditions that might mimic dementia. Brain Imaging is also used to detect any physical changes in the brain associated with dementia.

To navigate this diagnostic journey effectively, an interdisciplinary team of healthcare professionals works together to ensure a thorough, accurate diagnosis that is tailored to the patient's unique experience. This team includes general practitioners, neurologists, and geriatricians, who provide a holistic perspective on the complexities of aging and cognitive decline.

Receiving a diagnosis of dementia can be an emotional moment for both patients and their families. Healthcare professionals should provide clear and empathetic support and information that is both hopeful and actionable.

When the time comes, support services, such as memory care facilities, adult daycare centers, home health services, support groups, and counseling services, are available to provide the patient with medical, social, and emotional support. These services acknowledge the multifaceted nature of dementia care and recognize that supporting patients and caregivers requires a mosaic of resources that work together.

Dementia is a disease that requires a medical diagnosis. Too many times, patients and their families chalk up the patient's forgetfulness to old age, therefore they put off seeking medical help and an official diagnosis. But as we have learned, early detection and intervention can help slow the progression of the disease and lessen the severity of symptoms.

2.4 The Progression of Dementia: What to Expect

There is no "typical" with dementia. The disease manifests in different ways in different people. How the disease progresses and what stages the patient will go through differ greatly from person to person. One thing is constant ... gradual symptoms will become worse. Understanding this progression will allow caregivers to assist their loved one as dementia takes the person further away from what is familiar and what they are used to.

Early Stages

Memory lapses, known as mild cognitive impairment, are an early sign of dementia. However, people at this stage can still perform daily activities and complex tasks. While the cognitive impairment can be worrisome, it allows for some normalcy and serves as a bridge between the onset of dementia and being cognitively unimpaired.

As the disease progresses, individuals transition into early-stage dementia, where the signs become unmistakable. Tasks that once came easily, such as managing finances or driving to familiar locations, now trigger confusion and doubt. In conversations, the person may lose their train of thought, forget common words, or repeat themselves. The person and listener can become frustrated and confused.

Middle Stage

Mid stage dementia further deepens the impact of the disease. During this stage, there is a significant decline in cognitive abilities and independence. Memory loss becomes so pervasive that the patient forgets details about their life and fails to recognize loved ones' faces. The ability to perform basic tasks, such as dressing or bathing, declines, demanding a level of care that is both constant and compassionate. It is within this stage that the essence of the person seems to fade away, challenging caregivers to find and hold onto the fragments of identity that remain.

Final Stage

In the final stage, severe dementia, individuals require comprehensive care for nearly all aspects of daily life. Communication becomes limited, with language reduced to fragmented sentences or, in some cases, entirely lost. The patient's physical condition also declines, often confining individuals to bed or chair. In this stage, the patient may enjoy brief moments of recollection and connection, but these become more rare and precious, as their world shrinks to the immediacy of comfort, care, and companionship.

Caregivers must draw on their emotional strength, but also practical preparations in anticipation of the increasing needs of the individual with dementia. Legal and healthcare planning emerge as crucial components of this preparation. Establishing powers of attorney, both for healthcare decisions and financial management, and advanced healthcare directives ensures that the individual's wishes guide the course of care and decision-making, even when they can no longer articulate those desires themselves.

Beyond these legal preparations, discussing and documenting care preferences for the various stages of dementia with the patient fosters a sense of control and agency in a process that often feels out of control. These conversations are difficult yet necessary, as they clarify pathways that honor the individual's values and wishes. They also align family members and caregivers so that all parties are on the same page regarding the course of care. The potential for conflict will be reduced so that the patient enjoys cohesive, consistent support.

As dementia progresses, the role of the caregiver evolves, expanding to encompass not only the physical care but also the preservation of dignity, the advocacy for the individual's wishes, and the maintenance of a connection to the essence of who the person was, and, in moments of clarity, still is. This role, although challenging, is also an opportunity – an opportunity to assure your loved one that you will be there to care for them and help them manage the loss of their former life.

2.5 Fostering Acceptance: Moving Forward After a Diagnosis

The Path to Acceptance

When a loved one is diagnosed with dementia, it's common for families to feel overwhelmed and unsure of what to do next. Initially, many people may try to deny or ignore the situation, but eventually, it becomes clear that this is not a sustainable approach. Acceptance is an important part of moving forward, but it can be difficult to reach. It's a gradual process that involves coming to terms with the reality of the situation.

As you begin to understand the challenges of dementia, you will find that it's easier to move forward. Though it may take some time, once everyone involved accepts the situation, you will gain a sense of clarity and peace that will help you and your family cope with what's to come. When you accept the reality of dementia, you can focus on nurturing your relationship with the patient that goes beyond basic care and cognitive decline. You can lay a foundation of trust and security that will be so important later on.

Acceptance, in this context, is not synonymous with resignation but represents a profound adjustment to a new reality. Acceptance is not "giving up." It involves acknowledging the dementia diagnosis and its implications, while also recognizing that the patient has life still to live. That life should be as fulfilling and joy filled as possible. Learning about dementia, engaging with support networks, and, perhaps most critically, allowing oneself to mourn the anticipated losses can all help you and your family accept your loved one's diagnosis. By educating ourselves, talking openly, and reflecting on our thoughts and actions, you can slowly begin to let go of your denial and see things more clearly. You may not know exactly what the future will look like, but you will have accepted the fact that it will involve change.

Acceptance and Caregiving

As a caregiver, once you have reached a place of acceptance, your approach to caregiving takes on a sense of purpose and adaptability. Acceptance empowers you to tailor your strategies to the evolving needs of your loved one. It shifts the focus from loss to maximizing present capabilities. Caregivers who embrace acceptance find themselves better equipped to handle the challenges of dementia care, from managing symptoms to communicating effectively and making difficult decisions regarding care plans.

Letting Go of What Was

Integral to the journey of acceptance is the process of grieving the loss of the loved one's former self—a complex, deeply emotional process. After all, the person you know and love will likely undergo some profound changes brought on by dementia. He or she may not remember your shared experiences, inside jokes, tradition, or even who you are to them. It's not easy to see your parent, grandparent, or loved one this way and it's difficult to watch as the ties that united you with this person slowly disintegrate. This grief, while painful, is a necessary passage, allowing caregivers and families to reconcile with the alterations in personality, memory, and function that accompany the condition. Letting go of past expectations and preconceived notions of the person's identity allows you to reorient towards who your loved one is in the present.

This process of letting go does not negate the memories or diminish the significance of the person's past but rather, places the focus on nurturing the relationship in its current form. You, as a caregiver, can discover new ways of bonding with your loved one, bringing joy to their lives, and creating an environment of peace.

Embracing the Present

The act of embracing the present amidst the challenges of dementia care is both a choice and a practice, requiring intentionality and mindfulness. It calls for a conscious effort to anchor yourself in the immediacy of the current moment and make day-to-day experiences special. This mindfulness, an attunement to the 'now.' Caring for a loved one with dementia is tough, but there will be moments of spontaneous clarity, gestures of affection, and glimpses into the strength of the human spirit. These are the moments you should hang on to throughout your caregiving journey. Living in the moment requires you to be flexible, adaptable, and patient. Dementia is an unpredictable disease that requires grace and creativity. By focusing on the present, you can create an environment that emphasizes comfort, contentment, and care.

If your loved one is having a good day, you might take an impromptu stroll through the park to look at the spring flowers or the fall foliage. Or maybe you can put on some classic songs and dance around the living room. Depending on your loved one's level of cognition, you could play a simple card game or board game. Do you have a family member with a new baby or toddler? Invite them for a short visit. Your loved one will probably light up in the presence of an infant ... and it may even bring back memories from when your patient was a young parent.

Chapter 3

TAKING ON THE CAREGIVER ROLE

As I noted earlier, there are more than 11 million people in the United States working as unpaid caregivers to a family member with dementia. The majority of them are women. Why do they choose to take on the caregiver role? While there are numerous reasons, most of them fit into one of two categories – love or money.

Family members often assume a caregiver role because they want to ensure that their loved one is treated with dignity and respect, love and compassion. The dementia patient may want to remain in their home for as long as possible, only moving to a dementia care facility if absolutely necessary. You may choose to care for your loved one because you deeply care for them, are devoted to them, and want the opportunity to show them the same affection they showed you in the past.

Memory care facilities and full-time home healthcare aids are both extremely expensive. Many dementia patients simply don't have the financial resources to cover these expenses. Or, perhaps they have some money set aside, but they want to save it for the time when an assisted living facility is the only option.

Becoming a caregiver often means putting your own life on hold, albeit temporarily, while you see to the needs of your loved one with dementia. It may require you to leave your job or move.

> Catherine had been living out of state, working hard to support herself financially. When her mother was diagnosed with dementia, it quickly became clear that her father, who was also struggling with his own health issues, could not manage her care alone. As the only daughter and without a family of her own, Catherine decided to step in and help. Initially, she intended to assist temporarily until an alternative solution could be found. However, as time passed and her mother's condition deteriorated, Catherine became increasingly involved in her daily care. She took on responsibilities such as managing medical appointments, handling medication, and becoming attuned to her mother's needs. Ultimately, Catherine made the difficult decision to quit her job and move back in with her parents. She became her mother's primary caregiver, dedicating herself fully to her mother's well-being.

3.1 Rewards of Caregiving

Caregiving can be a tremendously rewarding experience, for both you and your loved one with dementia. Being a caregiver is an opportunity to:

- Give back to a loved one
- Show your loved one how much you love them
- Spend time with your loved one
- Make sure your loved one has joy and happiness in their life
- Give your loved one stability and familiarity

- Ensure that the patient is treated with compassion, respect, dignity, and empathy
- Learn more about your loved one
- Develop new skills
- Discover your underlying strengths
- Learn more about dementia, the healthcare system, and insurance/Medicare programs
- Appreciate life's journey
- Connect with other caregivers and spread awareness about dementia
- Hone your stress management, interpersonal communication, and self-care techniques

3.2 Challenges of Caregiving

The rewards of caregiving also come with challenges and obstacles. In fact, the main goal of this book is to help you address and overcome these challenges so your own mental and physical health does not suffer and so you can provide the best care possible to your loved one during this difficult time. Among the challenges of caregiving are:

- Frustration
- Depression and anxiety
- Feelings of isolation
- Sleep deprivation
- Physically strenuous
- Exhaustion
- Lack of privacy
- Lack of support from other family members
- Feeling taken advantage of
- Being afraid to ask for help
- Physical and emotional stress
- Financial strains
- Lack of personal time
- Loss of friends
- Inability to do the things you once loved to do

3.3 Types of Caregiving

The caregiver experience differs depending on your loved one's needs and if there are other caregivers involved. Because of the progressive nature of dementia, the situation may change and evolve over time. You may be a:

- **Primary caregiver** – You are either the only one caring for your loved one with dementia or the person who is responsible for the bulk of their care.
- **Secondary caregive**r – You are a part-time caregiver who helps the primary caregiver.
- **Member of a caregiving team** – You and several other caregivers share caregiving duties, taking turns helping your loved one.
- **Live-in caregiver** – You reside in the same home with your dementia patient, therefore you are available to help them around the clock.

3.4 Creating Joy and Meaning in Everyday Life

When it comes to taking care of people with dementia, finding happiness should be a daily practice. Your patient deserves to feel positive emotions despite their disease and you, as a caregiver, should not be forced to wallow in despair and negativity. You and your patient will both benefit from daily doses of happiness. The key is to focus on small moments of joy and fulfillment, rather than big gestures. Understanding of what brings happiness to your loved one with dementia. And, then, adding these to your patient's day.

Finding Joy in Small Moments

When people with dementia experience joy, it's often through simple, shared moments. These moments can be fleeting and unexpected, but they bring happiness and a sense of connection to the patient. Joy can come from things like feeling the warmth of sunlight in the morning, hearing a favorite song, or someone brushing their hair. These small moments matter a lot to people with dementia, because they help them feel more present and comfortable.

To create an environment where these moments can happen, it's important to pay attention to what the person with dementia likes and what engages their senses.

- Does your loved one light up when you serve him or her a cup of fragrant tea?
- Does he or she smile when hearing a familiar tune?
- Do you notice a sparkle in his or her eyes after putting up a colorful painting?

When people with dementia can engage their senses, they can enjoy everyday activities more, and find pleasure in new discoveries.

Activities to Enhance Quality of Life

Engaging in planned, structured activities can improve the lives of people with dementia. When people pursue hobbies and interests that align with their preferences and abilities, it can stimulate cognitive functions and bring purpose and pleasure to their daily lives. For example:

- Gardening is a great multisensory experience that provides a sense of accomplishment and wellbeing. It involves the tactile sensation of soil, the visual beauty of blooming flowers, and the responsibility of nurturing life.
- Music has the unique ability to evoke emotions and memories, which can spark moments of clarity and recollection.
- Art therapy helps individuals communicate through creativity and self-expression.

Customizing Activities

To get the most out of activities, it's important for you as a caregiver to tailor hobbies to align with your loved one's interests, abilities, and stage of dementia. This way, the activities won't just be engaging, but will also be accessible and provide a sense of accomplishment instead of frustration. Here are some suggestions:

- If your patient enjoys cooking, they can participate in meal prep, even if it's just washing vegetables or stirring a pot. This will help them feel like they are contributing.
- If your loved one loves reading, use of audiobooks or reading sessions that match their reading comprehension level can bring back the joy of storytelling and connect them to the stories they once loved.

To achieve this, it's important to keep assessing your loved one's preferences and capacities, and adjust activities as needed. In doing so your patient can gain a renewed sense of independence and identity, giving them control within their abilities and creating an environment where they can thrive.

Celebrating the Person's Legacy

Honoring the legacy of a person with dementia can be a meaningful way to celebrate their life. To do this, it's important to acknowledge their life story, talents, and accomplishments and include these in their care. You can share memories by looking through photos and keepsakes to reinforce your loved one's sense of self and create new connections with caregivers and family members.

Incorporating aspects of their career, hobbies, or passions into their daily routine can also help to remind them of their contributions and achievements. For example:

- If your patient used to be a musician, listening to their old recordings or incorporating music into their day can keep their passion alive.
- If your patient was an avid gardener, keeping a small indoor garden or arranging flowers can help them to stay connected to their interests.
- If your patient loves classic cars, plan a visit to a local car show.

This celebration of legacy can help to affirm the person's identity and worth beyond their experience with dementia. It's a practice that enriches their life and can also offer family and caregivers a deeper appreciation of their journey. By honoring their legacy, we can foster connections that endure through the challenges of the condition.

3.5 Educational Resources for New Caregivers

Most people step into the role of caregiver of a family member with dementia with no prior experience or education in this area. That's okay. You do not have to be a nurse or other healthcare professional to take on this challenge. But you should have a willingness to learn about caregiving. Fortunately, there are plenty of books on the subject, as well as classes and workshops designed to arm new caregiver's with an arsenal of knowledge. While you can certainly learn much of caregiving "on the job," so to speak, it's beneficial to have formal training in certain areas.

- The Alzheimer's Association has chapters in each state. Check their website for information about in-person and on-line training courses.
- Many hospitals offer training courses or workshops for family members of dementia patients. Check with hospitals in your area to see if there are any upcoming training sessions.
- Community colleges often have short, certification workshops for dementia caregivers as part of their course offerings.
- Contact any local dementia support group in your area. They should be able to point you in the right direction.
- Peruse the shelves of your local libraries and bookstores and you will find a variety of books dedicated to dementia care – practical how-to guides, reports on dementia research and treatment options, resource manuals, personal journeys of other caregivers, and memory-boosting exercises.
- Search the Internet to find articles, forums, and downloadable guides online. Websites maintained by reputable organizations dedicated to dementia research and care provide updates on

groundbreaking treatments and insights into the psychological and emotional aspects of caregiving.

You can make the best decisions for your loved one with dementia if you stay informed about new dementia research and innovative treatment developments. Subscriptions to newsletters from leading dementia research organizations, attendance at annual conferences, and active participation in online caregiver communities ensure that caregivers remain at the forefront of knowledge. Knowledge empowers caregivers like you to make informed decisions, advocate effectively for their loved ones, and adapt their care strategies to incorporate the latest findings.

3.6 Reflective Exercise: Mapping Your Caregiving Journey

Take a moment to reflect on your journey as a caregiver. On a piece of paper, create a simple timeline of your caregiving experience so far. Mark significant milestones such as the moment of diagnosis, memorable instances of joy and connection, and challenging periods or decisions. For each milestone, jot down a few words about how you felt, what you learned, and how it shaped your approach to caregiving. This exercise is not about dwelling on the past but about recognizing the depth of your journey, the resilience you've harnessed, and the love that has guided you.

In exploring the basics of dementia, we open a gateway to understanding the condition and the profound human experience intertwined with it. Dementia, with its myriad challenges and moments of clarity, teaches us about the resilience of the human spirit, the depths of compassion, and the enduring strength of love. As we move forward, let us carry with us the knowledge of the potential for extraordinary personal growth, learning, and profound connection that lies in the heart of caregiving.

Chapter 4

FAMILY DYNAMICS

Family dynamics exist in every family. Each person's unique personality, outlook, religious and political views, past experiences, and goals for the future are factors in how each member interacts with each other, what roles they take on in the family, and where they see themselves in the family hierarchy. The way family members communicate, cooperate, and handle conflicts can all significantly impact the care of a dementia patient. Positive family dynamics – clear communication, mutual support, and shared responsibilities – can lead to a more organized and compassionate approach to caregiving. However, negative dynamics – grudges, unresolved conflicts, sibling rivalries, one-upmanship, or unclear expectations – can create stress, lead to burnout, and potentially compromise the quality of care provided. Understanding and addressing family dynamics is essential for ensuring that your loved one with dementia receives the emotional, physical, and practical support they need.

4.1 Family Roles and Expectations

When a loved one is diagnosed with dementia, caregiving duties often fall to the patient's family. The roles assumed by family members can vary from primary caregiver to financial supporter to emotional anchor. Unless roles are clearly defined, discord and misunderstanding can arise. The challenge, then, lies not in the roles themselves but in the dialogue – or lack thereof – surrounding their adoption. Open conversations about each member's capacities and desires, along with an understanding of the dynamic nature of dementia care, can pave the way for a distribution of responsibilities that honors both the needs of the individual with dementia and the well-being of the caregivers.

4.2 Dealing with Conflict

When caregiving responsibilities are shared, conflicts are bound to pop up. It could be that someone is not pulling their weight or is shirking their duties. It could be that opinions differ on care strategies or financial management. The key to resolving conflict is to understand the different personalities and family dynamics that come into place, then concentrate on open, positive, productive communication with a willingness to compromise. You may have one or two family members who have take-charge, assertive personalities. These people tend to want to railroad their ideas through without putting things to a vote. Other family members may be much more passive. They prefer to sit back, have others make the decisions, and wait for someone to tell them what to do. You likely have a few family members who can't say "no". They are already over-extended with work, coaching their son's Little League team, organizing the PTA fundraiser, chaperoning school field trips, and volunteering at the homeless shelter. Yet, they eagerly volunteer for caregiving tasks. To work through your family dynamics, plan regular family meetings – by video-conferencing such as Zoom, if necessary – during which you can seek solutions and work toward collaborative action.

4.3 Family Meetings and Decision Making

It's not easy to have serious, uninterrupted discussions at family gatherings, like holiday dinners, birthday parties, or backyard barbecues. This is why it's important to have regular, structured family meetings to keep everyone informed about your loved one's care decision-making process. These meetings should cover care plans, financial arrangements, and the emotional toll of caregiving. Have clear agendas, allocate plenty of time for each topic, and make decisions that reflect the best interests of the individual with dementia.

4.4 Creating a Care Circle

Beyond the immediate family lies a broader community of potential support, a circle of friends, neighbors, extended family, and community members ready to lend their strength to the caregiving effort. Your loved one with dementia deserves a care circle that includes people who are important to them, whether they are related by blood or not. Reach out to these people to gauge their interest and willingness to help. Once you create a care circle, it operates as a second layer of assistance, offering practical help – from meal preparation to transportation – and emotional support that alleviates the isolation often felt by caregivers. The more clearly you can communicate your needs, the more you will be able to rally the care circle around your loved one in times of need.

There are unspoken dynamics in all families. To form an effective care team for your loved one with dementia, the caregiver roles should be clearly defined so you and your family members can focus on conflict resolution, collective decision-making, and mutual support. Open dialogue, empathy, and shared responsibility will ensure the well-being of the individual with dementia and strengthen the family as a whole.

Chapter 5

CREATING A DEMENTIA-FRIENDLY HOME

In most cases, a dementia patient remains in his or her home, or the home of a family member, for as long as feasible. The home – how it is arranged and what safety measures can be added – becomes important. The goal is to create an environment that upholds dignity and independence while promoting well-being and safety. By making practical adjustments to the home, you can keep your loved one in familiar surroundings where memory triggers abound.

5.1 Establishing a Safe and Comfortable Environment

Risk Assessment

Your first step in creating a safe, comfortable environment for your loved one with dementia is to evaluate the surroundings. This assessment should be careful and thorough, identifying any potential hazards that may be hidden in plain sight, such as:

- Loose rugs that could cause falls
- Cluttered areas that could obstruct movement
- Poorly lit corridors that could obscure visibility

By addressing these risks, you can make changes to the physical space that not only mitigate danger but also maintain a sense of familiarity for your loved one. Your goal is to keep your patient in the home as long as possible, therefore your evaluation and risk assessment should also consider future modifications that can be put into place when the time comes.

Creating a Dementia-Friendly Home

A dementia-friendly home is, first and foremost, one that is familiar and comforting to the patient. Be careful not to make too many or too drastic of changes at once, as this could confuse and overwhelm your loved one. Take it room by room.

The main living space, where the patient will spend most of the day, should have a simple, easy to navigate, floorplan. You want the patient to be able to get from Point A to Point B without having to negotiate his or her way around unnecessary objects. Consider:

- Removing items that aren't needed, such as tables or shelves stacked with knickknacks, extra chairs, large potted plants, or coffee tables.
- Make sure electrical cords for lamps or other items aren't stretched across walkways.
- Clear clutter off end tables so that your patient can have easy access to things he or she may need, like a glass of water, the TV remote, the telephone, and a book.
- Position your loved one's favorite chair so he or she can see the television without a glare from the window and in a place where he or she can see when people walk into the room. You don't want your patient to be startled, especially if he or she no longer recognizes friends and family.

Bathrooms and stairways are the two places where falls are most likely to occur. Implement strategies to reduce risks, such as:

- Installing safety bars in your patient's shower and, if possible, next to the toilet.
- Getting a toilet safety frame.
- Using a shower stool to allow your loved one to sit while showering.
- Install a walk-in shower, if possible.
- Using a swinging shower chair that can assist you in getting your patient into a bathtub when stepping over the edge becomes too challenging.
- Making sure that the bath mat or any rugs in the bathroom have slip-resistant backing or are held firmly in place with two-way tape.
- Installing handrails on one, or ideally, both sides of staircases.
- Adding additional lighting to stairways.
- Installing motion sensor lights around the stairs in case your patient wanders around in the night.
- Putting down easy to install anti-slip treads to hardwood staircases to reduce the risk of falls.

5.2 Use of Technology for Safety

Technology can be your ally in keeping your loved one safe. There are tools, devices, and apps that enhance safety and oversight while still preserving autonomy. For example: door alarms and video doorbells, like Ring doorbells, can offer you peace of mind because you can monitor your patient's coming and going without restricting their movement and freedom.

Personal safety monitors, like Life Alert, are helpful if your loved one is still mobile and doesn't yet require constant supervision. You will be alerted if your patient falls, needs assistance, or wanders off. Most brands have a tracking device built into them. If you download the company's app and set up a password, you can check your patient's location so you can make sure they are safe while allowing them to enjoy their autonomy. Apple's air tags are also helpful in tracking your loved one's movements.

If your loved one has a smartphone, there are several apps that can help improve their safety. GPS is a key one. It can help your loved one find his or her way to the grocery store, church, or a family member's house. Even though your patient may have gone to these places hundreds of times in the past, dementia can fog their brain and make them lose their way.

Carolina and her brother, Tomas, took turns checking in on their mother, Maria, who was in the early stages of dementia. They were concerned about Maria living alone, but she reassured them that she could handle it, just as she had for the last ten years since becoming a widow. Carolina and Tomas got a Life Alert for Maria, installed shower bars in the bathroom, and moved the washer and dryer to the main floor so Maria wouldn't have to go down the basement stairs. Maria always loved to cook big family meals for her extended family and still spent long hours in the kitchen. However, she often forgot ingredients in her favorite recipes. One day, when Tomas stopped by to check on his mother, he found her sitting in her recliner, staring off into space. The house was full of smoke, and the fire alarm was going off, but Maria didn't seem to notice. She had been cooking and forgot what she was doing, so she went to sit down, leaving the stove on and an oven mitt too close to the burner. The fire was already spreading to the curtains. If Tomas hadn't visited when he did, the house might have burned down, and Maria might have been injured or killed. After this incident, Carolina and Tomas installed an automatic shut-off device on the stove and arranged for Carolina's daughter, a college student taking online courses, to do her schoolwork at Maria's house. They also made a plan for the time when their mother would need a full-time caregiver.

5.3 Balancing Safety with Autonomy

Caregivers of individuals with dementia face a delicate balancing act of providing safety while maintaining independence. You don't want to offend your loved one by over-babying them or restricting their freedoms, but you also want to keep them safe. In the home, there are steps you can take to strike a balance between safety and autonomy. For instance, you could "shrink" the living space in your loved one's home by bringing the washer and dryer up from the basement, closing off extra bedrooms, and moving items stored on high shelves to floor level.

As your loved one begins to decline, both physically and cognitively, you may want to add more safety features to the home, such as a wheelchair ramp, door and window locks and sensor alarms to alert you if your patient opens them, safety gates at the top of stairs, and a whole-house video monitoring system. It may be necessary to install a lock on a kitchen cabinet to keep sharp knives, cleaning chemicals, medication, matches or lighters, and other potentially dangerous items out of the hands of your patient. By thoughtfully assessing risks, modifying living spaces, and using technology, you can maintain a safe, familiar home.

Chapter 6

HANDLING POTENTIALLY CHALLENGING SITUATIONS

As a caregiver of someone with dementia, you will experience many unique challenges. Your days and nights will be devoted to supporting the well-being of someone grappling with memory loss. This is a confusing, frustrating, and difficult time for your dementia patient and they may behave erratically and angrily.

You have the opportunity to create a meaningful and positive impact in your loved one's life during this painful and burdensome stage. The complexities of this condition can be frustrating and overwhelming for you, too, but with patience, empathy, and a willingness to learn, you can navigate the challenges and help your loved one feel loved and supported every step of the way.

6.1 Sundowning

At some point in your caregiving journey, you may encounter the phenomenon known as sundowning. Sundowning is a condition in which the dementia patient demonstrates increased confusion, agitation, and restlessness as daylight fades, or, as the name implies, when the sun goes down. Researchers have yet to unlock the root causes of sundowning but it's believed to be linked to a disruption of the circadian rhythm, the diminishing light, and the exhaustion from the day's stimuli, contributing to an escalation of symptoms associated with dementia. When your patient experiences sundowning, it can be upsetting to caregivers. It also poses some unique challenges.

To mitigate the effects of sundowning, a thoughtful approach that combines environmental adjustments with schedule modifications can offer relief. As a caregiver, you can try to uncover the stimuli that may contribute to agitation and strive to set a calm and soothing environment as evening approaches. Soft lighting, coupled with the reduction of noise and the introduction of familiar, comforting routines, can ease the transition into night. Activities that promote relaxation, such as listening to soft music or engaging in gentle physical exercises, can also serve as effective countermeasures against the restlessness that sundowning brings. You can also try to align the day's schedule to harness your patient's natural ebb and flow of energy – with more stimulating activities occurring earlier and a gradual winding down later in the day – to pave the way for a more peaceful evening.

Despite these interventions, there are moments when sundowning may become too profound for you to manage alone. Recognize when to seek professional help. Signs that indicate the need for expert intervention include persistent agitation that is not alleviated by environmental or routine modifications, significant alterations in sleep patterns leading to distress, and any behavior that poses a risk to the safety of the patient or others. Consulting healthcare professionals who specialize in dementia care can provide access to a broader range of strategies and possibly medication management to address these challenges.

As a 911 dispatcher working the night shift, Abbie has learned about the potential dangers sundowning poses to dementia patients and, believe it or not, to law enforcement officers. She has fielded frantic emergency calls late at night from people claiming a stranger was in their home or that someone was trying to break into their house. Naturally, when there are calls like this, the police are immediately dispatched to the scene. And they arrive with guns drawn, ready to capture the perpetrator. In reality, there are no intruders. The frantic call came from a dementia patient suffering from sundowning who either imagined the attempted break-in or did not recognize their caregiver and mistook them for a robber. This puts the caregiver in a dangerous position. The police may even detain the caregiver while they sort through the situation. The dementia patient is often agitated, frightened, and insistent that they are in danger. Since Abbie works in a small community, she has noticed that some dementia patients experiencing sundowning frequently call 911. She now keeps a list of known sundowning patients. When they call in the middle of the night in a state of agitation, she talks calmly to them to ease their minds. She still, of course, sends the police to the patient's home to assess the situation, but she informs them that it's the home of a dementia patient. Knowing this, they can approach the scene in a manner that keeps everyone safe.

6.2 Understanding and Managing Aggression

Identifying Triggers

Even in a patient with severe dementia, aggression often doesn't spring forth without reason. Warning signs and triggers are present, though they may be subtle or difficult to spot. Triggers can range from physical discomfort or pain, frustrating communication barriers, to environmental factors that overwhelm or confuse. As a caregiver, recognizing these triggers involves a careful observation of patterns – when and where do these episodes tend to occur? Is it during times of high activity or noise, or perhaps during personal care routines that might feel invasive? In addition to identifying these triggers, you will also need to address them proactively.

De-escalation Techniques

When signs of aggression begin to appear in your loved one with dementia, it's time to pull out your de-escalation tools. Try to:

- Maintain a calm demeanor
- Use a soft tone of voice
- Approach your patient from the front to avoid startling
- Stand close enough to communicate clearly, yet far enough to avoid feeling intrusive
- Empower your patient by providing them with a semblance of control, especially in a situation where they might feel powerless
- Redirect focus to a favorite activity or topic

Communication Strategies

Effective communication is the cornerstone of navigating aggression. As a caregiver, remember to:

- Avoid confrontation
- Speak in short and simple sentences
- Use non-verbal cues to convey understanding and compassion

- Validate their feelings even if the reality they perceive differs from your own
- Practice active listening
- Give them your full attention
- Acknowledge their concerns as this can often diffuse tension and show them that they are heard and valued

Self-Care for Caregivers

Once you have been able to de-escalate your patient's aggression or violent moment and defuse the situation, your loved one might feel better, but how about you? These encounters are stressful and unnerving. Acknowledging the toll these episodes take on you as a caregiver. That is the first step in self-care. Practice techniques such as deep breathing, mindfulness exercises, or even stepping outside for a few moments of fresh air to help reset the emotional baseline. Seeking support, whether through talking with friends, joining a caregiver support group, or consulting a professional for coping strategies, is essential. Remember, tending to your well-being is not just beneficial for you – it's crucial for the care recipient as well.

De-escalation Techniques

De-escalation techniques involve approaching calmly, maintaining personal space, offering choices, and redirecting focus. Active listening is key, emphasizing empathy and understanding. These methods aim to create a safe environment, reduce tension, and prevent conflict by fostering communication and acknowledging the person's feelings.

Figure 1: De-escalation Techniques

Navigating aggression in dementia care requires preparation, understanding the triggers, and employing de-escalation techniques with patience and empathy. Like any storm, these episodes do pass, and in their wake, the opportunity for calm and connection re-emerges. Let go of your own anger and do not hold a grudge. Remember – always – that your patient's emotions are being controlled by their condition. As hard as it can be, don't take their angry outbursts personally. Instead, practice effective communication and prioritizing self-care. Strengthen your resilience so you are ready to face the next challenge with compassion and understanding.

6.3 Wandering

The forgetfulness and confusion of dementia are rooted in the brain's faltering neurons. This can manifest, not only in profound confusion, but in wandering. The National Council on Aging reports that roughly 30% of dementia patients will wander. Your loved one with dementia may experience disorientation, fail to recognize once-familiar settings, have an altered sense of the day and time, or even forget their own identity.

In the cloud of confusion, your patient might leave home and wander the streets, aimlessly looking for something they can't even remember. As a caregiver, you will need to watch for signs of wandering in your patient and take steps to keep them safe.

Proactive Measures

Although it's vital to respect your loved one's need for autonomy, you, as a caregiver, should take a proactive stance to erect safeguards against the risks associated with wandering. This means anticipating potential scenarios and taking practical measures such as installing door alarms, and motion-activated security cameras. Identification bracelets are discreet yet informative and provide identification and the contact information of their caregivers in case a person with dementia wanders away from home. These measures can ensure safety.

Act Quickly

If your loved one with dementia goes missing, you, as a caregiver, must react swiftly. You can keep panic at bay by having a plan in place. Who will you call? Do you have a team in place to help you search the neighborhood? At what point will you contact the police? Does your loved one have a favorite spot he or she may go to? Do you have a current photograph of your patient that you can share with the police if necessary?

Time is of the essence when a dementia patient wanders away and becomes lost. Weather conditions – extreme cold or extreme heat – can be dangerous. If your loved one is exposed to the elements for too long, they may experience hyperthermia, dehydration, heat stroke, or frostbite. Likewise, the terrain surrounding your patient's home could pose hazards. Is the home near a busy highway? Are there abandoned buildings in the neighborhood? Are there bodies of water – ponds, streams, lakes, or the ocean – close by? Are there dense forests, deep ravines, desert areas, or rocky cliffs? When searching for a lost dementia patient, always start looking in the places that pose the greatest dangers. The confusion of dementia fogs your loved one's brain, making them believe they must urgently go somewhere. This is a key reason why they wander in the first place. If your patient wanders off, remember that they are not thinking logically. During your search for them, don't ignore areas that you think your loved one would avoid. For example, you may think "That swampy area is too muddy and stinky. My patient wouldn't venture into this area." They might!

Tips for Bringing Your Dementia Patient Home Safely

Once you track down your wandering loved one, you will need to take care in approaching them. You will be understandably relieved to find them and see that they are safe and you may be tempted to run up to them, give them a hug, and tell them you are taking them home. But take care. Most likely, they will not remember who you are or associate you with safety and love. You may frighten your loved one if you approach them too quickly or attempt to touch them. They may think you mean them harm or are trying to kidnap them. Instead, temper your excitement. Approach your patient slowly and calmly, speaking in a comforting and reassuring voice. Call them by name ... and tell them your name. Remind them who you are. If your patient is agitated, spend time calming them down before you attempt to get them in your car. In their state of confusion, they may resist, become aggressive, or try to run off. They could hurt you or themselves, especially if they dart into traffic or stumble and fall. Unless they are in immediate danger, take the time to assure them that you are helping them before you take action.

Connor just took on the caregiver role for his uncle, Mike, moving into his guest bedroom to give him round-the-clock care. One evening, Mike put on his jacket and shoes and told Connor he needed to go home. Connor explained that he was at home ... that he had lived there since the mid-1970s. But Mike became increasingly anxious, restless, and agitated. Connor went to the basement to put the laundry in the dryer. While he was down there, he heard the door to the garage slam shut. Connor dashed up the stairs in time to see Mike back his old truck out of the driveway and speed away. As quickly as he could, Connor slipped on his shoes and snatched his own car keys. Although Mike had a head start, Connor was able to see him several vehicles ahead of him. Suddenly, Mike pulled into a random driveway a few blocks away. By the time Connor caught up to him, Mike was on the doorstep of the home, trying to open the door. The residents were scared, but Connor explained that Mike was a dementia patient who was having an episode. Mike pointed to the pair of large, red flower pots flanking either side of the walkway, saying that he knew he was at his house because of the red flower pots. Connor and the homeowner let Mike touch the flower pots. By then, Mike had calmed down and allowed Connor to put him in the car. The kind homeowner even offered to drive Mike's truck home for them.

6.4 Communication Do's and Don'ts

Effective communication with your loved one with dementia lies not in the number of words exchanged but in the clarity and simplicity of your interactions. As your patient's condition deteriorates, it will demand a departure from conventional conversational norms.

Effective Communication Techniques

To avoid confusion, your conversations with your loved one should be clear and concise. For example:

- Sentences should be constructed with care, stripped of unnecessary complexity, and delivered slowly and patiently to allow the listener time to process and respond.

- Avoid using metaphors, overly descriptive language, or big words.
- Make sure each sentence conveys a single complete thought ... that your sentences are not too complex or fragmented.
- When you are explaining something to your loved one with dementia or giving them instructions, tell them one step at a time. It may be difficult for them to comprehend multiple steps when presented all at once.
- When you ask your loved one with dementia questions, pose them one at a time and frame them to elicit "yes" or "no" responses. Wait for an answer before asking the next question to prevent further confusion.

This simplicity in speech does not equate to diminishment in respect or consideration. You do not have to talk down to them or use baby talk. Rather, try to acknowledge their altered processing capabilities without compromising the dignity of the individual.

Avoid Arguing and Correcting in Communication

Arguing with a dementia patient is a fruitless endeavor that only serves to heighten your loved one's frustration and distress. Expect your loved one to say things that you don't agree with – even things they would never have said before dementia clouded their thoughts. Sadly, dementia diminishes logic and reasoning. No matter how much you argue, debate, and persuade your loved one, you will be fighting a losing battle. All you will be doing is creating tension, frustration, and confusion in your patient and yourself.

Similarly, avoid the impulse to correct inaccuracies. Your patient will mix up details, forget key facts, and merge two stories together. Accept this as part of the pitfalls of dementia. Though often well-intentioned, constantly correcting your loved one can lead to feelings of inadequacy and disorientation. As a caregiver, it's often difficult to refrain from correcting your loved one with dementia, but it's best to just let things go, for the sake of your patient's serenity.

Using Body Language and Tone

Posture, gestures, and expressions conveys intent and emotion without the need for spoken words. When interacting with your dementia patient, use a stance that is open, a gentle touch, and eye contact to communicate your presence, sincerity, and love. The tone of your voice, too, can calm, soothe, and reassure your loved one. You will need to be mindful of your actions, stance, tone, and body language so you can adopt a non-verbal communication habits that best suit your role as a caregiver.

Practical Communication Tips

The practicalities of daily communication with someone with dementia demand both creativity and adaptation. If your loved one can no longer use their words, you can try visual aids – a board or placemat with images of a TV, glass of water, toilet, etc. on it – so your patient can point to a picture of what they need. Simple photographs, symbols, and objects can trigger recognition and facilitate understanding, acting as anchors in conversations that might otherwise drift into confusion. When you offer short, segmented information that is coupled with the use of visual cues you can create a system for effective communication.

The Impact of Physical Touch

Never underestimate the power of a hand held in comfort, a gentle pat on the back, or a reassuring hug to communicate support, love, and understanding in ways words cannot. This tactile language, when used appropriately and sensitively, fosters a connection that nourishes both you as the caregiver and our loved one with dementia. All people crave human touch and interaction ... this is something that dementia doesn't steal from its victims.

As a caregiver to a loved one with dementia, physical touch provides a way to demonstrate your understanding and compassion. When you are mindful of how you touch your patient – whether it's to complete a care task or to offer a consoling, comforting gesture – you can fulfill their need for human touch in the most gentle way.

6.5 Techniques for Diffusing Difficult Situations

Throughout your dementia care journey, you will likely experience moments that test your mettle – situations fraught with tension, fear, and frustration. The key to navigating and defusing difficult situations lies in maintaining your composure and keeping a level head through the storm. The art of staying calm under such pressures is not innate; it's honed through practice and patience. The most seasoned caregivers will tell you that techniques such as deep, measured breathing, and remaining silent can ground the caregiver in the present and ward off panic. When you are calm, you can radiate this vibe to your loved one with dementia, offering reassurance and guidance.

One technique for diffusing tension is to redirect your dementia patient's attention away from the situation that is causing them distress. When you can recognize the person's likes, dislikes, and stress triggers, you can introduce a favored topic of conversation, or offer a cherished object to hold. These can serve as a diversion, drawing your loved one's focus away from sources of agitation and toward calmer grounds. The deftness with which this redirection is executed often determines its success. As a caregiver, you will quickly learn what works for your loved one. When you observe signs of tension and aggression in them, you will know what you can do to help soothe their emotions.

Distraction techniques are particularly beneficial because they are versatile and immediately effective. Consider playing your loved one's favorite music or initiate a simple, hands-on activity to distract your dementia patient and engage their senses and cognitive faculties in a manner that sidelines distress. This approach requires you, as the caregiver, to be tuned into triggers and subtle signs of impending aggression so you know when to introduce the distraction for maximum effect.

There may be moments when your best efforts to diffuse and distract your loved one with dementia simply isn't enough to quell a difficult situation. In these instances, your best course of action may be inaction. Retreat and give your patient space and time to find solace on their own. Take a step back from the situation – and from your loved one – to allow their emotions to work themselves out and their perspectives to shift. This brief separation gives both you and your dementia patient a few moments to gather yourself, clear frustrations, and re-emerge renewed. Everyone needs a break from the people closest to us every now and then. Just make sure that your loved one is left alone in a safe, secure environment and that they aren't left alone for too long. You want them to know that you will continue to be there for them ... even if they need to let off some steam from time to time.

Employed with sensitivity and adaptability, distraction and diffusing strategies give caregivers like you tools to handle difficult situations.

6.6 Strategies for Managing Public Outings

Your loved one with dementia will benefit from venturing beyond the familiar confines of home. In addition to attending doctor's appointments, going to place of worship, and visiting friends, your loved one may enjoy going out for lunch, strolling through a park, or attending a concert or sporting event. These excursions are potentially enriching and can add to your patient's quality of life, but as a caregiver, you will need to make meticulous preparation to navigate public outings successfully. Here are some suggestions:

- Carefully pick the destination and the timing of the outing to make sure that it aligns with your loved one's interests, energy level, ability, and cognitive understanding. For example, you may want to plan your outings for mornings, when your dementia patient's energy levels are at their zenith and the crowds at your destination haven't reached their peak.
- The noise and crowds can cause dementia patients to become disoriented and distressed. To mitigate these challenges, anticipate your patient's response and be prepared to deploy your calming techniques and diversionary tactics.
- Try employing noise-canceling headphones.
- Having a familiar, comforting item on hand can serve as effective tools in maintaining equilibrium amidst the din.

- Safety should be your top priority during public outings. Incorporate identification methods, such as wearable ID bracelets or tags sewn into clothing, to ensure that you can be quickly reunited with your loved one should you become separated.
- GPS tracking devices, such Apple air tags, can be discreetly placed in pockets or accessories, allowing caregivers to monitor the whereabouts of their loved ones without encroaching on their sense of autonomy.
- When you and your loved one with dementia arrive at a public place, establish a clear, easily recognizable meeting point.
- Bring a companion to help you, when possible. Ask a family or a friend to join you on the outing.

Yet, for all the planning and precaution, things sometimes go wrong. That is the unpredictable nature of dementia. The ability to modify plans as circumstances evolve is crucial. Maybe it is making the decision to cut an outing short when signs of fatigue or distress emerge, or altering the day's agenda to accommodate the shifting moods of the person with dementia. To keep your loved one safe, you must be willing to adjust the day's experiences around the needs and comfort of your patient. It also means setting aside your own expectations for the outing and staying attuned to your patient's state of mind.

Outings are beneficial for many dementia patients. While there are challenges and safety concerns, you can mitigate them with meticulous preparation, an unwavering commitment to safety, and the willingness to adapt. It may be tempting for caregivers to avoid taking their dementia patient out in public, however getting out of the house can provide them with opportunities to engage with the world in ways that are meaningful, enjoyable, and secure.

As a caregiver, your role in managing public outings includes navigating the challenges of crowds and noise, ensuring safety, and championing flexibility.

Chapter 7

DEMENTIA TREATMENTS AND MEDICATIONS

A dementia diagnosis typically means frequent doctors' visits, various medical tests, and a cache of medications. Caregivers like you end up juggling appointment calendars, maintaining medication schedules, watching for side effects, and accompanying your loved one to medical visits. It requires you to have an understanding of dementia treatments and medical options so that you can advocate for your patient when they cannot advocate for themselves. From pharmaceutical interventions to non-pharmaceutical strategies, dementia treatment's path is fraught with decisions, requiring not just a keen understanding of the options available but also the ability to converse with doctors and insurance companies.

7.1 Understanding and Accessing Dementia Treatments

Overview of Treatment Options

Dementia treatments are as diverse as the individuals they aim to support. Often, it involves a blend of pharmaceutical and non-pharmaceutical approaches. On one hand, medications such as cholinesterase inhibitors and memantine offer a way to manage symptoms, potentially improving quality of life by enhancing cognitive function or mitigating behavioral changes. On the other hand, non-pharmaceutical interventions – ranging from cognitive stimulation therapy to lifestyle modifications like diet and exercise – can be a crucial part of your patient's holistic care.

Accessing Care

The caregiver's role includes guiding the dementia patient through the complex healthcare terrain. There will likely be a primary care physician overseeing the patient's care, with referrals to specialists, such as neurologists, geriatricians who specialize in dementia, speech and physical therapists, dieticians, and more. These specialists are equipped with a deep understanding of dementia's nuances and can offer insights into the most effective treatment plans. Beyond the clinical setting, community resources such as support groups and advocacy organizations that provide information and support to help caregivers and their loved ones with dementia to make informed decisions about care.

The Role of Care Plans

A comprehensive care plan, co-created with healthcare providers, is a guide to the dementia treatment process, offering a detailed map of the care journey. This plan is tailored to your loved one's specific needs and stage of dementia and outlines both the medical and supportive care strategies for optimal well-being. It's a dynamic document, evolving as the needs of the dementia patient change, ensuring that the care provided remains aligned with their current status and long-term goals. As a caregiver, your input in the care plan's development is vital. After all, this plan is a collaborative effort, involving not just the healthcare team but also the person with dementia, and the "boots on the ground" ... you and any other caregiver.

7.2 Common Medications

Thanks to advances in modern medicine, there are several medications that can temper the symptoms of dementia. Among these, cholinesterase inhibitors—such as Donepezil, Rivastigmine, and Galantamine – offer a ray of hope. This family of drugs works to slow cognitive decline by bolstering communication between nerve cells. Yet, there are potential side effects, ranging from nausea to the more severe, like bradycardia (when your heart rate is slower than normal). Memantine, which navigates a different path, operates by regulating the activity of glutamate, a chemical involved in information processing, storage, and retrieval of information in the brain. Side effects of this medication can span from dizziness to agitation. As a caregiver, it's vital that you understand these medications, their intended benefits, and their potential effects, as well as the dosing amounts and schedule.

7.3 Medication Management

The act of managing multiple medications can be a tricky one that demands precision and attention to detail. This is why caregivers like you need to take control of the storage, refilling, and administering of all of your dementia patient's medications. Some medications can interact negatively with each other, so they cannot be taken together. Others work best when taken with food, while some should be taken on an empty stomach. You will need a strategy for medication management, such as making a comprehensive medication list that includes not only prescription drugs but also over-the-counter remedies and supplements. This document becomes a reference point for healthcare providers and caregivers alike.

Implement a system of reminders, be it through the use of pill organizers or digital alerts, to guard against missed doses or doubling up. If there are other caregivers involved, make sure they are aware of your medication management system and know how to use it. Lastly, safeguard your dementia patient's medications by storing them in a locked area. In the confusion of dementia, patients often insist that they have not taken their morning meds even though they have, or vice versa. If your loved one has access to their medication, they may take too many pills or take the wrong ones.

7.4 Communicating with Healthcare Providers

Healthcare providers use their education and experiences to develop a "big picture" approach to dementia care, but they are not "in the trenches" with you, the day-to-day caregiver. The doctors rely on you to provide insights and observations that can shape the trajectory of your loved one's individual treatment. Too often, people are intimidated when talking to doctors, afraid that they will sound stupid – because, among the older generation, doctors have a reputation for being really, really smart – or that their concerns won't be taken seriously. Doctors are smart, but they don't know your loved one like you do. Communicate openly with your loved one's healthcare team. Give them your nuanced observations and details so they have the information they need to make the best decisions for your dementia patient. For every appointment, arm yourself with observations, questions, and concerns, and present them with clarity. Provide supporting evidence, such as notes or a journal in which you have documentation of symptoms and side effects. As a caregiver, you are the voice of your patient. Your communications and interactions with healthcare providers should be your opportunity to advocate for your loved one and create a collaborative approach to treatment adjustment and optimization.

7.5 Alternative Medications and Supplements

Medications extend beyond traditional pharmacology and prescription drugs. There are also over-the-counter medications, alternative medications, and supplements. Alternative medications and supplements promise relief or improvement through means that are not always anchored in scientific research. It's not uncommon for people to assume these alternatives, from herbal remedies to vitamin supplements, are safe to use because they are natural. Yet, the natural compounds with herbal medications and supplements are still potent and powerful. They need to be used with caution to reduce the risk of undesired side effects or harmful interactions with other medications. Remember that you and the healthcare providers and partners in the care of your loved one. Keep them informed of any venture into the world of alternative treatments, ask for their guidance when selecting herbal remedies, and discuss the latest scientific evaluations of alternative medicines with them. There is certainly a place for alternative medicine, but it should work in conjunction with traditional medicine, not against it.

As a caregiver, you stand as both navigator and advocate. It's up to you to understand the broad spectrum of treatment options and master the intricacies of care access and insurance navigation. Additionally, the proper use of medications can slow dementia's progression and give your loved one more moments of clarity. As a caregiver, you will be tasked with administering your patient's medications, keeping to dosing schedule, and watching for potential side effects. Frank, honest discussions with your patient's healthcare providers will help you and your dementia patient understand the medicine that has been prescribed.

Make a Difference with Your Review

Unlock the Power of Generosity

"Sometimes, the smallest act of kindness can make the biggest difference."
- Anonymous

People who give without expectation live longer, happier lives and feel more fulfilled. So, if we can make a difference together, let's give it a shot!

To make that happen, I have a question for you...

Would you help someone you've never met,

even if you never got credit for it?

Who is this person you ask? They are like you. Or, at least, like you used to be. Less experienced, wanting to make a difference, and needing help, but not sure where to look.

Our mission is to make dementia caregiving easier for everyone. Everything I do stems from that mission. And the only way for me to accomplish that mission is by reaching...well...everyone.

This is where you come in. Most people do, in fact, judge a book by its cover (and its reviews). So here's my ask on behalf of a struggling caregiver you've never met:

Please help that caregiver by leaving this book a review.

Your gift costs no money and less than 60 seconds to make real, but can change a fellow caregiver's life forever. Your review could help...

...one more family provide better care for a loved one. ...one more person find strength in their caregiving journey. ...one more caregiver feel less alone. ...one more reader discover helpful tips and support. ...one more dream of compassionate care come true.

To get that 'feel good' feeling and help this person for real, all you have to do is...and it takes less than 60 seconds... leave a review.

Simply scan the QR code below to leave your review:

https://www.amazon.com/review/create-review/?ie=UTF8&channel=glance-detail&asin=B0DCP82PV8

If you feel good about helping a faceless caregiver, you are my kind of person. Welcome to the club. You're one of us.

I'm that much more committed to help you provide the best care possible. I'm hopeful that you will benefit from the strategies and support I'm about to share in the coming chapters.

Thank you from the bottom of my heart.

Suniti Barua, PhD

PS - Fun fact: If you provide something of value to another person, it makes you more valuable to them. If you believe this book will help a fellow caregiver, send it their way.

Chapter 8

WORKING WITH HEALTHCARE PROFESSIONALS

When caring for a dementia patient, caregivers like you are forced to wear many hats. In addition to being a day-to-day caregiver, you will also become an advocate, strategist, and record-keeper. It's a balancing act that is not always easy, but you can keep everything running smoothly by being organized and prepared when interacting with healthcare professionals, engaging in effective communication, being diligent about follow-up, and including your loved one with dementia in conversations about their own care. It's a dynamic process, but you can take steps to achieve the best possible outcomes.

8.1 Getting the Most from Your Medical Appointments

Appointment Preparation

Prepare for upcoming medical appointments with your loved one with dementia. This preparation goes beyond simply collecting medical records. It involves detailing your questions, observations, and documents to support a fruitful dialogue with your loved one's healthcare providers. This includes:

- Any recent health developments with your dementia patient – changes in behavior, cognitive abilities, or physical well-being – along with dates, situations, and specific details to provide a clear picture of their current state to their doctor.
- A list of all medications – prescription, over-the-counter, herbal medications, and supplements – to give your patient's healthcare provider a comprehensive overview of potential interactions and side effects.
- Questions you compile. Don't worry about asking a "stupid" question. In the world of dementia care, there are no stupid, embarrassing, or silly questions. The physicians on your loved one's healthcare team have heard it all before. They won't laugh at you; they will admire your purposeful intent to advocate for the best possible care for your loved one.

Effective Communication Tips

Often, healthcare appointments involve a barrage of information that, in the moment, can be so overwhelming that you don't have time to process everything in order to ask effective questions. As your loved one's caregiver and advocate, your task is to decipher the new information while also getting your pre-written questions answered. It can be a lot. One of the best ways to make this exchange of information go smoother is to frame your conversations with healthcare providers to be clear, concise, well-supported, and assertive.

Articulate your concerns without equivocation, and present observations and questions with confidence. After all, you have a more intimate understanding of your loved one with dementia's condition because you live it every day. Employ active listening when communicating with healthcare providers. If you did not understand what they said or you had trouble hearing any part of it, ask the doctor to repeat the information or explain it to you in layman's terms.

Follow-up and Record-Keeping

Keep careful notes about follow-up care and record information after each appointment. Develop a system for documenting all relevant information that can be easily accessed and reviewed as needed. This practice serves to ensure continuity of care and can guide future care decisions. This involves not just the recording of medical advice and prescribed treatments but also the detailed notation of any recommended changes to care routines or lifestyle adjustments. Such records become invaluable over time, offering a view of the person with dementia's health journey, allowing for the evaluation of treatment efficacy and the identification of patterns in symptom progression. It will help you juggle the various appointments and compartmentalize the information you are getting regarding your loved one's disease progression. Good record-keeping also helps other caregivers involved in your loved one's care, as well as the patient's family members.

With so much information going back and forth, it's easy to miss something. Ask your healthcare provider if you can record the appointment using the voice memo record feature on your smartphone. They will almost always agree. You then have an audio record that you can refer back to later, when you are trying to sort out the details of the appointment. You can play back all or part of the recording with your dementia patient, depending on their level of cognitive understanding, so they are kept abreast of their healthcare journey. You can also share the recording with other family members and caregivers, so everyone involved in your loved one's life is kept in the loop about medical developments. Lastly, you will be able to transcribe the recording and include it with your journal, binder, or folder of healthcare information for your dementia patient.

Involving the Person with Dementia

As always, you want to respect and involve your loved one with dementia in their care decisions and medical appointments. It acknowledges their personal rights, autonomy, and dignity. During appointments, however, stay attuned to your loved one's capacity for understanding and participating. You want to be sensitive to their cognitive and emotional state. It validates their experiences, ensuring that their voice, however diminished by the condition, is heard in the decisions that shape their care. Even in instances where your patient's direct participation might be limited, the symbolic act of including them in these processes reinforces to them that they still have some control in their lives, despite dementia.

8.2 Building a Healthcare Team

During your loved one's journey through dementia care, he or she will assemble and collaborate with a multidisciplinary healthcare team. This team of expertise, ranging from primary care physicians to specialists in neurology and geriatric care, forms the cornerstone upon which comprehensive care rests. The role of caregiver requires you to have an acute understanding of the varying roles each member plays in your loved one's healthcare plan but also a commitment to fostering an environment of cooperation and mutual respect between you, your dementia patient, other caregivers, and the healthcare team.

The initial steps in forming this alliance involve professionals who not only possess the requisite expertise but also exhibit a willingness to engage in a truly collaborative partnership. You want healthcare professionals on your team who are compassionate, empathetic, and will listen to your questions and concerns. This selection process, though daunting, is informed by consultations, recommendations from trusted sources, and, importantly, personal interactions that gauge each potential member's rapport, approachability and commitment to patient-centered care. Once assembled, this team becomes an invaluable resource for you as a caregiver – true partners in your care of your loved one with dementia.

8.3 Seeking Second Opinions

Your commitment to securing the best possible care for your loved one with dementia may mean that you want to seek second opinions regarding their health care. That's perfectly acceptable. In fact, it's never a bad idea to get a second opinion. Dementia is a complex condition with numerous treatment options. A second opinion may offer confirmation or an alternative perspective. As a caregiver, you should have an understanding of when and why such consultations are warranted, be it due to uncertainties about the diagnosis, concerns about the proposed treatment plan, or simply for peace of mind. Seeking a second opinion does not mean you distrust your loved one's healthcare provider. Rather, it's a proactive step in ensuring that the care strategy embraced is comprehensive, evidence-based, and tailored to the individual's evolving needs.

8.4 Handling Hospital Stays

There may be times during your caregiving journey when your loved one requires a hospital stay. It could be due to a planned procedure or because an emergency situation – an accident or illness – has happened. If you have a plan in place for hospital stays, you can make these incidents less stressful and confusing for your loved one while also ensuring continuity of care. Maintain a binder with your loved one's essential medical history, current medications, health insurance information, living will, and current treatments that you can bring with you to the hospital. You can also include your loved one's specific needs, preferences, and potential triggers for distress. Communicating effectively with hospital staff, from nurses to specialists, demands clarity, assertiveness, and persistence, ensuring that the care provided within the hospital setting reflects the patient's unique circumstances.

Your loved one with dementia may experience the most agitation and distress during transitions – from home to the hospital, from hospital to home, or from hospital to another care facility. Your presence during these times can be reassuring to your dementia patient – a familiar face and voice amid the chaos. When you attend these moments, you can also make sure you completely understand the discharge instructions and that follow-up care is seamlessly integrated into the ongoing care plan.

The healthcare professionals caring for your loved one with dementia are a key part of the support team. Selecting these team members is a dynamic process. It requires continuous engagement, informed advocacy, and an unwavering dedication to securing the best possible outcomes for your dementia patient. It's the role of caregivers to wield the tools necessary to forge a dementia care plan.

8.5 The Role of Specialist Care: Geriatricians and Neurologists

Your loved one with dementia will be seen by geriatricians and neurologists, each bringing their expertise to dementia care. These specialists offer insights into specific aspects of dementia. Geriatricians, for example, focus on the aging process. They concentrate on optimizing the quality of life for older adults by addressing health concerns that intersect with dementia, from comorbid conditions to the subtleties of age-related physiological changes. Neurologists, on the other hand, delve into the neurological underpinnings of dementia, decoding the signals of cognitive decline in the brain's architecture and the nervous system's pathways. Together, these specialists form a crucial alliance in the care team, ensuring a plan that is both precise and person-centered.

At what point in your dementia patient's journey do you need to add geriatricians and neurologists to their care team? Identifying the opportune moment to weave these specialists into the care demands keen observation and a proactive mindset. There may be signs, subtle shifts in cognitive abilities, or a behavioral pattern that deviates from the norm. These signals are your cue to seek the help of specialists to uncover the underlying causes and potential interventions that can mitigate the progression or impact of dementia. Your loved one's disease progression will dictate when and if it's necessary to fortify the care team with experts, such as geriatricians and neurologists, that can complement and enhance the existing dementia care strategies.

Geriatricians and neurologists enrich the overall dementia care approach. Their expertise, when added to the efforts of the broader care team, offers strategies that are nuanced, targeted, and deeply respectful of the individual's journey with dementia.

8.6 Research and Clinical Trials: What's on the Horizon

The world of dementia research is evolving fast, with new discoveries and advancements emerging every day. The latest scientific discoveries hold the promise of transformative treatments and care strategies. At the forefront are clinical trials. These innovative trials can give us glimpses into the potential future of dementia care.

Current Dementia Research

Before we can look at where dementia care will be going in the future, we need to understand the current knowledge and treatment options. Data gleaned from molecular biology, neuroscience, genetic, and psychosocial studies are giving researchers a better view of the human brain. Scientists are exploring the genetic markers and molecular pathways that point to dementia with the goal of unlocking targets for novel therapeutic interventions. Concurrently, work is being done on non-pharmacological approaches, from cognitive rehabilitation exercises to dietary modifications. This multifaceted approach enhances the patient's quality of life and manages their dementia symptoms.

Participating in Clinical Trials

For families touched by dementia, clinical trials are as much about contributing to the collective quest for knowledge and solutions, as they are about prolonging the life of their loved one. Before jumping into a clinical trial, however, you need to carefully evaluate the potential risks and weigh them against the benefits. As a caregiver, this decision should not be yours to make alone. Depending on your loved one's level of cognitive understanding, they should have a voice in the matter, as should family members.

The next step would be finding suitable clinical trials, a task that demands discernment and an understanding of the criteria for participation. Once you find an appropriate clinical trial, the decision to participate should be made after a thorough understanding of the trial's aims, the interventions involved, and the implications for the individual's care.

The Future of Dementia Care

Ongoing research and clinical trials, coupled with innovations in pharmacological treatments, show promise in slowing disease progression or alleviating symptoms in dementia patients. Emerging technologies, from wearable devices that monitor health metrics to artificial intelligence applications that support cognitive function, hint at a future where dementia care is both personalized and pervasive.

Staying Informed

In the swiftly evolving landscape of dementia research, staying informed is both a challenge and a necessity. As a caregiver, you can acquire information from a variety of resources – academic journals, research newsletters, conferences, webinars dedicated to dementia care. Armed with knowledge, you, as the caregiver, and the patient's family can make informed decisions about care and treatment.

As a caregiver of a loved one with dementia, you should strive to stay abreast of new advancements in dementia research, or, if appropriate, include your dementia patient in clinical trials. Several different scientific disciplines are directing research into the causes, prevention, and treatment of dementia.

Chapter 9

BASIC CARE FOR YOUR DEMENTIA PATIENT

The task of caregivers is to provide basic care for their loved one with dementia. As I will detail in this chapter, basic care includes serving them a proper diet, ensuring they get physical exercise, adopting good sleep and hygiene habits, and practicing mental stimulation activities.

9.1 Nutrition and Meal Preparation Tips

Simplifying Mealtime

Caregiving can be overwhelming, especially when it comes to mealtime. But there's a way to make it simpler, less stressful, and more enjoyable for both you and the person with dementia. For example:

- Prepare meals that are easy to cook and packed with nutrition.
- Meal prep by spending one afternoon a week to cook and prepare meals for the whole week.

- Pre-portioned meals and meal kits take away the guesswork over measuring ingredients, allowing the dementia patient to feel more in control.

Sensory Considerations

The senses of taste and smell for individuals with dementia can be affected in subtle yet profound ways. This might not be something you thought of before, however you can enhance meals by offering contrasting flavors in food, as well as visually appealing presentations. Your loved one may be more inclined to eat.

Assistance and Independence

Caring for individuals with dementia requires a delicate balance between offering assistance and encouraging independence, especially during meal times. As a caregiver, you should try to be sensitive to the person's changing abilities and to observe non-verbal cues indicating their need for help or desire for self-reliance. There are ergonomic designs of adaptive eating utensils on the market that can allow your loved one to continue self-feeding even as their motor skills wane. And, the way you position food on plates can be instrumental in enabling ease of access and reaffirming their dignity.

Hydration Strategies

Hydration is essential for good health for everyone, but it can be difficult for people with dementia. The key is to make drinking fluids more appealing. You can try:

- Offering flavored water or herbal teas, which are tasty and enjoyable.
- Reminding your patient to drink fluids by placing visual reminders where they can be seen.
- Serving foods with high water content, such as soups, fruits, and smoothies, can also help.
- Try popsicles if your loved one is comfortable with the cold temperatures.

- Investing in insulated tumblers with lids and built-in straws that will keep water cold longer and aren't easily spilled.

By making hydration part of daily life, you can help people stay healthy without making it feel like a chore.

9.2 Personal Hygiene: Best Practices for Dementia Care

Maintaining a Hygiene Routine

Personal hygiene is more than just being clean. For a person with dementia, it can also be a task that makes them acutely aware of their loss of dignity and self-esteem. Creating a consistent hygiene routine for your patient requires not only respecting their dignity, but understanding their preferences and being sensitive to their abilities and comfort. It's a deeply personal and humbling activity that can be made less awkward if you, as the caregiver, strive to maintain the respect of your patient through each step of the process, from brushing hair to toweling off after a bath.

Adapting Hygiene Tasks for Independence

Personal hygiene tasks can make your patient feel dependent on others. However, there are some helpful products that can improve independence and make daily routines easier. For example:

- Electric toothbrushes
- No-rinse bathing products
- Clothing with Velcro closures and elastic waistbands designed to help people with declining motor skills to take care of themselves

These modifications can make a big difference in preserving your loved one's self-esteem and autonomy.

Handling Resistance to Hygiene Care

Your loved one with dementia may resist hygiene care not because they are stubborn, but because they are afraid, confused, and want to maintain their independence. To approach this resistance, caregivers must understand the patient's perspective and use empathy, creativity, and patience when broaching the subject. You can try offering your loved one choices, such as:

- Choosing a bathing time or toothpaste flavor,
- Selecting the songs you will play during hygiene time to make the experience more pleasant
- Explaining each step of the task in a calm and reassuring tone

Privacy and Dignity in Hygiene Care

When caring for your loved one with dementia, it's important to respect their right to privacy and dignity, especially when it comes to personal hygiene. This respect is shown by taking actions that protect their sense of self and maintain their privacy to the highest possible degree. Try simple techniques such as using bath blankets while bathing or dressing in a way that minimizes exposure to maintain their modesty. It's essential to approach conversations about hygiene with sensitivity and without judgment, so your loved one with dementia feels valued and understood.

9.3 A Restful Night's Sleep

A restful night's sleep is crucial to the well-being of dementia patients, however sleep often becomes elusive due to sundowning, agitation, and confusion. Establish a consistent bedtime routine and talk to your loved one's other caregivers to make sure everyone follows the same routine. Maintaining a fixed schedule for sleeping and waking keeps the body's internal clock stable.

You should also make sure your loved one's sleep environment is conducive to rest. Ask yourself:

- Is the bed comfortable?
- How about the blankets, sheets, and pillows?
- Is the temperature in the room ideal for sleep?
- Is it quiet and free of stimulations?
- Many people have televisions in their bedrooms. For a dementia patient, this might interrupt sleep patterns and cause agitation.

9.4 The Importance of Routine in Dementia Care

Creating a Daily Schedule and Routine

Establishing and maintaining routines can create a sense of comfort, familiarity, and predictability for your loved one. By providing them with a structured framework, you can anchor their experiences in the familiar and lessen the cognitive load required to navigate each day. Following a routine can help reduce instances of confusion and distress, allowing your loved one to engage in activities and rest with reassuring consistency.

Meaningful rituals, such as enjoying a morning cup of tea or taking an evening walk, can also bring joy and serenity to their day. To build such a schedule, it's important to understand your loved one's natural inclinations, preferences, and their life patterns before the onset of dementia. By observing their peak alertness and times of restfulness, you can tailor activities and rest periods to align with their natural rhythms.

Flexibility within Structure

As much as structure and routine are important when caring for a loved one with dementia, the disease can cause unpredictable changes in cognitive and physical abilities. As a caregiver, you also need to be flexible. When confusion or fatigue is overwhelming, you will have to adjust the schedule – shorten activities, take longer breaks, or skip tasks altogether. This does not mean abandoning the routine entirely, but rather adapting to your patient's current situation. It's about making sure that the schedule serves the individual and not the other way around.

Involving the Patient in Planning

In dementia care, it's important to recognize your patient's agency and right to participate in the decisions that shape their lives. By involving them in planning their daily routine, you empower your patient and reaffirm their autonomy within the confines of their condition. This collaborative approach ensures that the schedule reflects your patient's preferences and interests. You should offer choices without overwhelming your loved one and respect their current capabilities while honoring their past selves. This approach dignifies and respects the person with dementia, acknowledging them not as passive recipients of care but as active participants in their journey.

In dementia care, a daily routine is a cornerstone of compassionate caregiving. It provides a sanctuary of normalcy and predictability. The routine should be crafted with care, flexibility, and an unwavering commitment to the individual's well-being. Through meaningful rituals and the active involvement of the individual in their care, caregivers illuminate the path forward. In this light, individuals with dementia navigate their days as captains of their ship, guided by those who walk beside them. Every thoughtful adjustment and every shared moment of joy honors their journey.

9.5 Creative Engagement: Activities for Body, Mind, and Soul

When caring for individuals with dementia, it's important to include creative engagement, physical activity, and social interaction. These activities support not just physical well-being, but also cognitive and emotional health. By recognizing the value of creativity, movement, and socialization, you can plan activities that mitigate the effects of dementia and enrich your loved one's days.

Benefits of Physical Activity

For those navigating the complexities of dementia, physical activity can help fend off the negative impacts of the disease. The physiology behind this is clear and compelling; regular physical activity stimulates not just the muscles but also the brain, encouraging the flow of blood and oxygen that nourishes neural pathways, potentially slowing cognitive decline. Moreover, the rhythmic nature of movement, from the steady steps of walking to the fluid motions of tai chi, brings about a sense of calm, stabilizing mood swings and fostering a state of mental equilibrium. The benefits extend into the realm of rest. Physical exertion often means a more restful and profound sleep.

Benefits of Creative Engagement

Creative activities engage the neurons in the brain and help strengthen pathways that have become eroded by the effects of dementia. Painting, drawing, needlework, and craft making serve as conduits for expression that stimulate neural pathways. The process of engaging creatively can provide your loved one with dementia an anchor to the present, a focus for their attention, and reduce the agitation that often accompanies the condition. Additionally, the act of creating something new imbues your loved one with a sense of accomplishment and purpose.

Incorporating Social Interaction

Incorporating social interaction into the daily activities of your patient with dementia combats isolation that too often accompanies the condition. Group activities – exercise classes tailored to the abilities of those with dementia or art sessions designed to foster creativity and camaraderie become spaces where dementia patients can share laughter. Everyone benefits from the presence of others, including dementia patients. Spending time with fellow dementia patients, family members, or caregivers reinforces your loved one's sense of self and diminishes the loneliness that dementia can bring.

Adapting Activities

The unique ups and downs of dementia demand that the activities your patient engages in be adaptable, evolving with the individual's needs and abilities. This adaptation ensures that activities remain not just accessible but also enjoyable, regardless of the stage of dementia. In the initial stages, activities might be complex, engaging your patient's cognitive and physical abilities fully. But, as the condition progresses, these activities might become too taxing. As a caregiver, you might need to help your loved one transition to simpler, less complex variations of their favorite activity. For example, you can guide your patient from painting detailed landscapes to experimenting with finger paints. The key lies in recognizing your patient's current abilities to ensure that every activity, no matter how adapted, continues to offer a sense of achievement and pleasure.

As a caregiver of a dementia patient, integrating creative engagement, physical activity, and social interaction will improve your patient's mind, body, and spirit. This approach offers individuals with dementia opportunities to celebrate the abilities and maintain human connections.

9.6 Stimulating the Mind: Cognitive Activities and Games

Because dementia targets the brain and creates cognitive decline in patients, games and activities that stimulate the mind can slow down the decline and engage your loved one's thinking process. Activities such as puzzles, board games, watching sporting events, playing memory games, and listening to music are not mere pastimes but vital elements of a care strategy designed to nurture the cognitive abilities of your loved one with dementia.

Cognitive stimulation, in its essence, taps into the brain's adaptive potential, the neuroplasticity that allows for growth and learning regardless of age or condition. These activities enhance memory, language, and problem-solving skills that may become obscured by the progression of dementia. Games and activities that stimulate the brain in your patient also foster a sense of achievement, provide a structure for social interaction, and most importantly, offer a conduit to memories and capabilities.

For caregivers and loved ones, the array of activities that can serve this purpose is vast and varied. Each one triggers different aspects of the brain. These include:

- Puzzles which demand the patient recognize patterns and understand spatial reasoning.
- Memory games – like those that involve remembering and matching cards or recalling and repeating lists – that stimulate the recall processes and provide a gentle workout for the brain's memory functions.
- Watching a sporting event, either live or on television, because it sparks the brain to anticipate outcomes and analyze strategies.

To maximize the benefits of these cognitive activities, you will need to make them adaptable to the abilities and interests of your loved one with dementia. As the disease progresses, your patient's ability to focus and complete tasks will change. Adaptable activities can change with your patient. A 1000-piece puzzle may have once offered hours of focused engagement, but now a simpler jigsaw puzzle evokes a sense of nostalgia. Similarly, memory games can be adjusted in complexity, from matching simple shapes and colors to recalling sequences of events or items, each variation tailored to the cognitive level of the individual. Music and art, too, can be easily adapted.

Engaging in meaningful activities, those that resonate with your patient's history, preferences, and sense of self, is crucial. These activities serve as cognitive exercises, giving your loved one's brain a workout. For someone who spent their life immersed in music, listening to favorite pieces or engaging in simple instrument play can awaken a profound sense of self. For an avid gardener, engaging in activities that involve plant care can provide a sense of purpose and a connection to their past. These activities, when chosen with care and consideration, affirm your loved one's identity and life experiences, offering a sense of accomplishment and belonging that is invaluable.

In the crafting of an environment that prioritizes cognitive stimulation, you can become the architect of a daily routine that integrates brain exercises, creating opportunities for engagement and connection. Through these efforts, you not only provide support for the cognitive needs of your loved one with dementia but also foster activities that become stepping stones towards well-being.

Chapter 10

LEGAL CONSIDERATIONS IN DEMENTIA CARE

Legal documents stand in for the dementia patient when they can no longer advocate for themselves.These documents ensure that their wishes and rights are upheld even when words fail them. In this chapter, we delve into the essential legal documents for dementia care, navigating the intricacies of protecting a loved one's rights, and outlining strategies for estate planning and asset protection. These legal frameworks, while possibly daunting at first glance, serve as the bedrock for securing a future that respects the dignity and wishes of those with dementia.

10.1 Key Legal Documents

Navigating dementia care requires a map of legal documents as diverse as the condition itself. Wills and trusts ensure personal wishes are respected posthumously, while powers of attorney and advanced healthcare directives speak on behalf of individuals when they no longer can. Reviewing and updating these documents is crucial, adapting them as circumstances evolve. Legal advice becomes indispensable in this process, providing clarity and direction through the legal jargon that often clouds these essential tools.

Protecting the Rights of the Person with Dementia

Imagine a scenario where a person's ability to communicate their healthcare wishes diminishes. Here, advanced healthcare directives act as their voice, articulating desires for treatment or declining specific interventions. This document is not merely about medical care; it's a statement of autonomy, ensuring the person's rights and preferences are front and center, respected by all. In moments where decisions are clouded by emotion and stress, this document stands firm, a testament to the person's wishes.

Estate Planning and Asset Protection

The cost of dementia care spirals like a vine, often unexpected and overwhelming. Estate planning and asset protection strategies become the shears to manage this growth, ensuring assets are shielded from the high costs of care while securing the financial future of the person with dementia and their family. Trusts, in particular, play a pivotal role, offering a flexible and protective mechanism for asset management. For example, a special needs trust can provide for the person with dementia without jeopardizing their eligibility for public assistance programs. This strategic planning transforms a potential financial burden into a managed aspect of dementia care.

The Role of Trusts

Trusts are like containers, holding assets under specific conditions for the benefit of the person with dementia. They vary in form, each tailored to different needs and outcomes. A revocable living trust, for instance, allows for the management of assets during the grantor's lifetime, with provisions for dementia care woven into its structure. On the other hand, an irrevocable trust can be used to set aside assets, protecting them from being counted against Medicaid eligibility thresholds. Understanding the nuances of each trust type is crucial, enabling families to choose the right container for their unique circumstances, safeguarding assets while ensuring care needs are met.

Checklist for Legal Preparedness

A comprehensive checklist serves as a guide for families navigating the legal aspect of dementia care. Including items such as:

- Consult with a legal professional specializing in elder law.
- Complete a will and review it annually.
- Establish a durable power of attorney for finances and healthcare.
- Create a living trust to manage assets effectively.
- Complete an advanced healthcare directive and discuss it with family members.
- Consider setting up a special needs or irrevocable trust for asset protection.

This checklist ensures no stone is left unturned in preparing for the legal challenges dementia care presents. It encourages proactive engagement with legal tools, ensuring the well-being and rights of the person with dementia are paramount.

Legal documents and strategies form the framework that supports not just the person with dementia, but their entire family. They encapsulate wishes, protect rights, and secure assets, ensuring the patient's dementia care is handled with dignity and respect. Through careful planning, informed advice, and strategic use of legal tools, families can build a foundation that withstands the challenges dementia brings, safeguarding the present and future for their loved ones.

10.2 Financial Planning for Long-Term Care

When your loved one receives a dementia diagnosis, one area of concern is the financial impact. The cost of dementia care can be overwhelming for families. No one wants to sacrifice the level of care because of financial constraints. Navigating this financial landscape includes understanding of the resources available, from the initial stages of home care to the possible transition into assisted living or skilled nursing facilities. Dementia care has a unique set of costs. Caring for your loved one at home, in a familiar and comfortable surrounding, may initially seem more financially manageable but this scenario can rapidly escalate as needs intensify. Assisted living, viewed as a middle ground, balances independence with available support, yet its cost can vary widely depending on location and services required. Skilled nursing facilities provide the most comprehensive level of care but represent a significant financial commitment. Understanding these costs is the first step in financial planning, a step that demands clarity and a willingness to confront the realities of long-term dementia care.

Financial planning guides families through their caregiving options. A budget for the care of your loved one should be put in place. It should be as realistic and comprehensive as possible, covering all current expenses and anticipating future ones. You and other family members will need access to the personal savings and retirement accounts belonging to your loved one with dementia so, with their permission, these funds can be used to pay for their care. Additionally, your loved one with dementia may potentially qualify for benefits and government programs. Long-term care insurance is designed to alleviate the financial burden of comprehensive care. Policies vary in coverage and cost, so it's imperative that you scrutinize the fine print.

If your dementia patient is eligible for Medicaid, you may be able to get paid for being their caregiver. Medicaid's Home Help program allows a family member or friend to become a paid caregiver for their loved one with dementia. There are some stipulations – the caregiver must be 18 years or older and legally able to work in the United States, for example.

Contact the Medicaid office in your state to determine your eligibility and for information on applying for the Home Help program.

Managing and protecting your loved one's assets is part of the financial planning process. Asset management in the context of dementia care transcends mere financial advice; it means ensuring that resources are allocated not just for immediate care needs but with an eye towards future demands. Protecting assets, such as real estate and investments, becomes a balancing act to maximize your loved one's resources while maintaining their eligibility for crucial support programs such as Medicaid. This endeavor is complex and has legal implications, so you may need to seek the expertise of financial planners or eldercare attorneys. These professionals are adept at navigating the care needs of dementia patients with their financial resources and legal constraints.

The importance of consulting with financial planners or eldercare attorneys specializing in long-term care planning cannot be overstated. These professionals have experience and a deep understanding of the financial and legal landscape of dementia care. They can serve as invaluable allies in your caregiving journey. Collaborating with these specialists offers families assistance with funding the patient's healthcare expenses and applying for assistance programs.

No one wants to let money dictate the level of care their loved one with dementia receives, but the reality is that healthcare and day-to-day care costs money. As a caregiver, you have options to explore and experts to consult to help you with the financial considerations of dementia care.

10.3 Understanding Guardianship and Power of Attorney

The sad reality of dementia is that your loved one will reach a point when they cannot make decisions for themselves. When that happens, they can still ensure that their wishes are known if they have a power of attorney or guardianship in place. As a caregiver, you should understand the differences between these two documents. Each one has its unique set of responsibilities, implications, and legal bearings.

Guardianship, which acts as a protective shield, is a court-appointed role, granting you – or another family member – the authority to make decisions on behalf of an individual who has been deemed unable to make those decisions themselves.

This legal instrument ensures the person with dementia's well-being and rights are meticulously safeguarded. Power of attorney, in contrast, is a proactive designation, a trust placed in you or another chosen individual to act on another's behalf, typically before the full impact of dementia unfurls. This preemptive measure assigns specific areas of decision-making power – from financial management to health care directives – to you or another family member.

The establishment of guardianship or power of attorney should not be taken lightly. It should be made after contemplation, legal counsel, and often, conversations with others involved. To establish guardianship, you will be required to go through the court system to present evidence that the dementia patient is incapable of making sound decisions for themselves. On the other hand, power of attorney can be drafted with legal guidance and specify the scope and limits of the agent's power. The person chosen to be the dementia patient's representative, be it for guardianship or power of attorney, must be trustworthy, able to advocate, and respect the person with dementia's values and desires.

Sadly, some family members have been known to take advantage of the cognitive decline of a loved one with dementia. From time to time, you will hear stories of how a family member tricked a dementia patient into handing over all their savings, changing their will, or signing over the deed to their home. Hopefully, you never encounter this situation during your caregiving journey, but it is wise to have safeguards against misuse of guardianship or power of attorney. This protection takes the form of oversight. For guardianship, the courts monitor the arrangement, which can serve as a deterrent. Regular reporting is a requirement of guardianships and ensures transparency and accountability. Power of attorney do not operate under the watchful eye of the courts system, however there are legal provisions in place that allow for the power to be revoked should abuse be detected, and recourse through legal channels to address any breaches of duty. These safeguards have been woven into the legal framework and protect against the exploitation of those with dementia.

10.4 Advanced Healthcare Planning for Dementia

Understanding Advanced Directives

Advanced directives are legal documents that serve to guide decisions based on the individual's values and wishes. These legal instruments include living wills, do not resuscitate (DNR) orders, and healthcare proxies are declarations of one's desires concerning medical treatment in situations in which their voice might be silenced by illness. The living will specifies the extent of medical intervention desired, and the healthcare proxy names a trusted individual to make healthcare decisions for the patient if the patient cannot make them.

Although these are legal documents, you do not need to hire a lawyer to draw up these documents. You can simply download the forms online. Once they are filled out, signed and dated, you will need to take them to a notary public to be notarized to make them legally binding. Copies of the advanced healthcare directives should be kept in your binder or folder along with other pertinent documents so they can be quickly located when needed.

Making Decisions about Future Care

The unpredictable nature of dementia makes planning for the future a challenge. There are medical factors that come into play, along with emotional and ethical quandaries. These decisions also include end-of-life care. This can be a delicate subject ... one that demands a sensitive, informed, and compassionate approach. No one likes to talk about the inevitability of death, but you will need to have some difficult conversations with your loved one – before their disease progresses too far – to ensure that their wishes and values are considered. An honest, practical, courageous, and open talk will allow you, as the caregiver, insight into your loved one's preferences when their condition declines.

Do they want to remain in their home as long as possible or move to an assisted living facility? When do they want to use palliative measures? The role of palliative care – emphasizing comfort and quality of life – becomes a focal point in these discussions, as it often aligns with the desire to avoid overly aggressive treatments in the disease's advanced stages.

When you know your loved one's wishes, you will be better able to make decisions that respect their desires. These conversations, though difficult, are necessary. They offer an opportunity to explore the full spectrum of care options, from home-based interventions to specialized dementia care facilities, weighing each against the backdrop of your loved one's desires and the realities of their condition. By proactively addressing these decisions, your loved one's care team and family can move forward in a way that respects the dementia patient's wishes, ensuring that the care received resonates with their values and preferences.

Communicating Wishes with Family

Keeping the lines of communication open always makes situations easier, including dementia care. This includes your dementia patient's immediate family. Family dynamics often come into play which is why it's imperative that the patient's healthcare preferences and care decisions are clearly communicated to everyone involved. As a caregiver, you will need to keep everyone up to date on your loved one's condition, but also understand their emotions and concerns. They may still be processing their grief over the diagnosis or feel guilty that they cannot help with caregiving duties. Perhaps they are stressed because they live too far away to be directly involved or are overwhelmed with their own challenges. When you take their emotional states into consideration, you will be better equipped to keep communications with family members positive and focused.

This dialogue should be initiated early in your loved one's dementia journey, allowing ample time for everyone involved to reflect and understand. Schedule one or more family meetings and bring in healthcare professionals or mediators when necessary. Having a structured and dedicated setting for these conversations – not just a few side conversations while enjoying Thanksgiving dinner – will ensure that all voices are heard and that the focus remains on honoring the individual's wishes.

While upholding the desires of your loved one with dementia should be the top priority, the dementia care path sometimes gets muddied when too many voices with differing opinions get involved. By proactively communicating with all family members to keep everyone informed about the patient's wishes, healthcare decisions, and advanced directives, you will be laying a foundation that minimizes the potential for future conflicts.

Chapter 11

PAYING THE COST OF DEMENTIA

Ongoing doctor care, medical tests, and home healthcare equipment are costly. Medical bills add up quickly. As a caregiver, you may be responsible for making sure your loved one's medical bills are covered by the appropriate insurance program, be it private insurance, Medicare, or Medicaid.

11.1 Understanding Medicare, Medicaid, and Insurance

Depending on your loved one's age and financial situation, they will likely have Medicare, Medicaid, and private health insurance. Each of these can be quite complicated. While trying to arrange the financial aspect of your loved one's dementia care, you will need to be able to decipher the coverage and eligibility so you can make strategic maneuvers to secure assistance funds for dementia care. Between governmental programs and private insurance policies, you may have to fight your way through a labyrinth of guidelines, restrictions, and forms, but it will be worth the struggle to ensure your loved ones receive the care they deserve.

Medicare and Dementia Care

Medicare – the government's promise of support for those aged 65 and over – presents a paradox of coverage in the context of dementia care. While it encompasses a spectrum of medical services, there are notable gaps in coverage for things you might expect to be a standard part of comprehensive dementia care. Hospital stays, doctor's visits, and certain rehabilitative services are included under Medicare, yet long-term care – a critical component of dementia support – is not. This coverage gap requires families to take a strategic approach to leverage Medicare's offerings for acute and short-term needs while seeking alternative avenues for the sustained, long-term care that dementia often demands. Medigap, and similar supplemental policies, have recently emerged to help bridge this gap.

Medicaid Eligibility and Benefits

Contrastingly, Medicaid offers a lifeline for long-term dementia care, including custodial and home health services. Eligibility for this program, however, is linked to financial criteria. Depending on your loved one's assets and how they have been managed, they may not qualify. The process of becoming eligible is daunting. Families must find the sweet spot between asset preservation and program qualification, a task that often involves consultations with elder law attorneys. Medicaid's Estate Recovery Program, a provision allowing for the posthumous recoupment of care costs, adds a layer of complexity.

Long-Term Care Insurance

Long-term care insurance is different from traditional health policies in that it specifically addresses the costs associated with long-term care services, including those required for dementia support. Families considering this route must carefully consider the policy offerings, weighing the benefits against the premiums with a discerning eye. Key considerations include the daily benefit amount, benefit duration, and the inclusion of inflation protection – factors that determine the policy's adequacy in covering future care needs.

Navigating Insurance Claims

The filing and management of insurance claims, whether under Medicare, Medicaid, or private long-term care policies, can pose challenges to you as a caregiver. Your dementia patient may receive denials or rejections from their insurance company. When this happens, you will need to open disputes or file appeals on their behalf. This is when the importance of good record-keeping and a document management system become clear. The appeal process often requires persistence and, at times, the assistance of healthcare advocates or legal professionals. Armed with evidence and a clear understanding of policy provisions, you can advocate for your loved one with dementia to ensure that their claims are covered.

When it comes to dealing with insurance companies, your caregiver's duties extend to being an advocate. Medicare, Medicaid, and long-term care insurance greatly reduce the financial burden of health care costs, but you may have to jump through a few hoops during the process.

11.2 Financial Aid and Assistance Programs

There are additional sources to help ease the financial burden associated with dementia care. These include assistance programs, community resources, and veterans benefits. Each of these has their own application process.

Government Assistance Programs

Government assistance programs offer a spectrum of financial support options, each designed to alleviate the burden of dementia care costs. These programs, from Medicaid to state-specific initiatives, provide a lifeline for families grappling with the financial demands of long-term care. However, gaining access to these resources can be challenging, as eligibility criteria and application procedures may differ. Each one has its own financial, medical, and residency requirements. To get the most out of these programs, it's important to take a proactive approach. As a caregiver, you need to understand the eligibility guidelines so that you can gather the necessary documentation and navigate the application process effectively. It's possible to unlock access to crucial support services ranging from medical care to home-based assistance, allowing your family to provide for your loved ones with the care they deserve.

Community Resources and Charitable Programs

Community resources and charitable programs also offer financial aid and services to individuals with dementia and their caregivers. These local or regional resources provide a patchwork of support that can range from respite care services to financial assistance for medical supplies and adaptive equipment. Tapping into these resources requires an understanding of the local landscape. You can contact area community centers, non-profit organizations, councils on aging, and dementia care networks. If they don't have their own programs in place, they can certainly point you to ones in your community. The value of these resources lies not only in the immediate financial relief they can provide but also in their ability to connect families with a broader support system.

Veterans Benefits

For individuals who have served their country in one of the branches of the military, the Department of Veterans Affairs (VA) should be your first stop when seeking additional sources of funding to care for your dementia patient. The VA has programs that encompass a range of services including healthcare, long-term care, and financial assistance specifically designed to address the challenges posed by dementia. Set an appointment for you and your loved one to meet with a benefits provider at your local VA to get assistance accessing these benefits.

Navigating the Application Process

The application process for financial aid and assistance programs is often lengthy and challenging. Take your time to fill out the applications correctly and include all required documents. Success in accessing these resources sometimes hinges on how thorough and well-supported the application is. Begin by assembling the documents you need to present the full scope of your loved one's medical condition, care needs, and financial status. This preparation, while laborious, helps streamline the application process, mitigating the likelihood of delays or denials due to incomplete or inaccurate information. Yet, even with thorough preparation, the application process can present obstacles. Carefully read the program's requirements so you can most effectively communicate your loved one's needs and circumstances. It's here that the value of persistence becomes evident ... you may have to appeal a denial or seek external support to advocate for their application's approval.

Support for dementia care can also include government assistance programs, community resources, and veterans' benefits. Don't let the hassle of the application process deter you from applying for these programs. Each one offers solutions to alleviate the financial burden of care, providing families with the means to secure the necessary services and support for their loved ones. The trick to navigating the application process is to be proactive, prepared, and a persistent advocate for your loved one with dementia.

11.3 Planning for Future Care Needs

How do you predict the future needs of your loved one with dementia? How can you prepare for their inevitable decline? The future is unpredictable and the unique nature of dementia makes it difficult to know what the future will look like. As a caregiver, your keen observation of the individual's current capabilities and challenges, coupled with an informed understanding of how the disease typically advances, will help you navigate into the future. You can take much of the guesswork out of the equation by having regular and ongoing consultations with healthcare providers who can help shed light on potential future needs based on clinical experience and the individual's health status. Such assessments are not static; they require periodic revisiting to adapt to the person's changing condition, ensuring that care plans remain responsive and relevant.

The time may come to consider moving your loved one with dementia to a long-term care facility. This is never an easy decision to make. There are both emotional and practical implications. How do you pick a long-term care facility that aligns with your loved one's wishes and your goals for their care? You will need to look at the types of care each facility provides, the costs, and the quality of care before making your decision. Additionally, you should get input from your loved one's other caregivers and family members. Together, you can schedule visits to potential facilities to gauge the atmosphere, observe interactions between staff and residents, and assess the adequacy of support services. Additionally, you can discuss the cost structures and explore avenues for financial support so you can make a sustainable choice.

Advance care planning is vital in preparing for future care needs. The process must be practical and logical to balance the emotional aspects of these decisions and your loved one's end-of-life wishes. Documenting your loved one's preferences ensures they are honored, and establishes a guide for caregivers, family members, and healthcare providers as the disease progresses. This planning is not a one-off task but an ongoing conversation, evolving as circumstances change and new considerations come to the fore.

The involvement of family in care planning and decision-making processes ensures that the burden of decisions and care does not rest on a single pair of shoulders. Even though you are your loved one's caregiver, you do not have to face these decisions alone. Communicate openly with family members to keep them up-to-date on concerns as your loved one's disease progresses. Call family meetings when needed to discuss your loved one's declining condition and your shared goals for their care. This not only strengthens the support network around the person with dementia but takes the responsibility of decision making off your plate.

As we close this chapter, we reflect on the challenges of planning for future care needs – needs that balances the immediacy of current care with the foresight required to traverse the path ahead. It's a journey paved with assessments, choices, and ongoing conversations, but each step taken should be done so with the goal of maintaining a continuum of care that honors your loved one's preferences and provides for their needs with compassion and dignity.

Chapter 12

AVOIDING SCAMS AND EXPLOITATION

Dementia patients, in their confusion, memory loss, and diminished logic, are vulnerable to scams and exploitation. Some of these threats come from outside sources ... professional scammers who prey on the elderly. Others, however, come from the inside ... friends, acquaintances, and family members who cloak their deception in the guise of assistance. As a caregiver to a dementia patient, you need to be on the lookout for these malevolent tactics so you can safeguard the personal and financial information of your loved one. If you see fraud or exploitation or suspect your loved one with dementia has fallen victim to a scammer, what should you do? Know the avenues for reporting and how to seek recourse to protect your dementia patient.

12.1 Recognizing Scams and Exploitative Tactics

The first line of defense against exploitation is the ability to discern the telltale signs of scams. For starters, these scams – which range from fraudulent investment opportunities to phishing attempts disguised as legitimate communications from financial institutions – share common threads of urgency, secrecy, and promises of disproportionate gain. For individuals with dementia, the challenge of recognizing these red flags is compounded by cognitive impairments. Con artists and crooks know this which is why they target the most vulnerable members of society with their manipulation and coercion tactics. As a caregiver, you must remain vigilant and keep current about the latest con targeting the elderly.

12.2 Protecting Personal and Financial Information

In an age where information is both currency and commodity, the protection of personal and financial data becomes paramount. This is especially true when our financial information is online. Robust cybersecurity measures, including the use of strong, unique passwords and the enabling of two-factor authentication on financial accounts, can offer some degree of protection against unauthorized access. But with dementia patients, there is an increased risk of them sharing sensitive information with the wrong people, thus putting themselves at risk for data exposure. If your loved one with dementia is still able to answer telephone calls, talk to them about the dangers of giving out their passwords to anyone over the phone, even if they sound like an employee of the bank. Perhaps you could post a note near the telephone to remind your loved one not to disclose personal information to anyone who calls. You may also need to manage and monitor access to financial documents and accounts, ensuring that personal details are divulged only when absolutely necessary and under circumstances of trust and security.

Most of Cathy's family dislikes her husband, Alvin. During a family meeting about Cathy's mom, Lorraine's dementia care, Alvin snooped through her mail and took a photo of her retirement account statement. He set up an online account using his email and phone number, pretending it was Lorraine's contact information.

Months later, Amy, Lorraine's main caregiver, discovered the unfamiliar contact details on the account. After calling the number and reaching Alvin's voicemail, she contacted the financial company to remove his access and provided a power of attorney proving she was in charge.

At the next family meeting, Amy confronted Alvin, warning him that his actions were illegal and she would press charges if he interfered again.

12.3 Reporting Suspected Scams

If you suspect that your loved one with dementia has become the victim of a scam, take swift and immediate action. Reporting these incidents not only aids in the pursuit of justice and the potential recovery of lost funds but it also prevents others from being targeted by the same scammer. Contact your local law enforcement, financial institutions, and consumer protection agencies as each of these plays a distinct role in the response to financial exploitation. Furthermore, reaching out to organizations dedicated to elder abuse prevention can give you guidance and support.

12.4 Legal Recourse

According to "Financial Exploitation in Aging: What to Know & What to Do," by Leslie Kernisan, MD MPH, fraud or exploitation of a dementia patient could include:

- Forging a dementia patient's signature
- Asking a dementia patient to sign a blank check
- Using a dementia patient's bank card of ATM card without permission
- Using a power of attorney to access a dementia patient's funds for personal needs
- Pressuring a dementia patient to loan out money or pay expenses for someone else

If you witness or suspect that your dementia patient has been swindled – even if it's by an opportunistic family member – report the incident right away. You should immediately:

- Talk to your dementia patient – listening to their side of the story helps them feel heard and empowered
- Your local Adult Protection Services office
- Collect and document information or evidence
- Contact the dementia patient's bank or financial institution – the 2018 Senior Safe Act makes it easier for banks to investigate suspected financial abuse of an elderly person
- Contact the police
- Make other caregivers and family members aware of the situation and ask if they have observed any suspicious activity

For victims of scams and financial exploitation, there is legal recourse as a way of seeking redress and accountability. Legal recourse requires a series of actions, from the filing of civil suits to recover lost assets to the pursuit of criminal charges against perpetrators. A legal professional who specializes in elder law and financial exploitation can help you and your loved one through the legal process. An attorney could even help pursue alternative dispute resolution mechanisms, such as mediation, as a pathway to resolution that may be less adversarial.

Chapter 13

BANISHING CAREGIVER BURNOUT

There is nothing simple or easy about being a caregiver to a loved one with dementia. It's physically and emotionally exhausting work – after all, you will be assisting your dementia patient as they move around the house, go to the bathroom, climb into bed, and attend various medical appointments. In between these activities, you will be preparing meals, doing laundry and housekeeping, and being a companion to your loved one. It's also emotionally draining to be your loved one's caregiver. You will witness their day-to-day struggles and cognitive decline. In "Caregiver Burden: A Clinical Review" the authors of the study note, "Caregiver burden is frequently overlooked by clinicians." The report goes on to state, "Risk factors for caregiver burden include female sex, low educational attainment, residence with the care recipient, higher number of hours spent caregiving, depression, social isolation, financial stress, and lack of choice in being a caregiver." Caregiver burnout is evidently real. What can you do to prevent it from happening to you? And if it does, what can you do about it?

13.1 Recognizing the Signs of Caregiver Burnout

Burnout creeps in slowly and is often mistaken for mere tiredness at the beginning. Yet, it's the type of tiredness that does not go away after a good night's sleep. Instead, it turns into chronic fatigue, irritability, and a pervasive sense of being overwhelmed.

Early Indicators

Constant fatigue, in fact, is one of the early indicators of caregiver burnout. The second one is irritability. Tasks you once approached with patience now seem annoying and insurmountable. You may feel overwhelmed by the demands on your time and energy. Recognizing these signs early – acknowledging how you feel – becomes crucial in preventing the full descent into burnout.

Emotional and Physical Symptoms

Burnout manifests as a combination of emotional turmoil and physical ailments. You may feel lost, hopeless, and alone in your caregiver journey. Symptoms of depression may cloud your job as a caregiver. You may experience anxiety, sleep deprivation, and health issues. If left neglected, these symptoms of burnout become more pronounced. For caregivers, self care requires first recognizing the symptoms of burnout before you can take steps to tackle them.

Impact on Caregiving

The quality of the care you provide to your loved one with dementia can be negatively impacted by burnout. Tasks become burdens, and your connection with your loved one may fray. You may be more frustrated and irritated. Your state of mind is detrimental to the happiness of the person in your care.

Acknowledging Your Limits

In a culture that often glorifies endurance, acknowledging one's limits is an act of courage. Recognizing when you have given more than you can give and seeking help to bring things back into balance is not showing weakness, being dramatic, or being selfish. It is, instead, being proactive about your mental health and taking the appropriate steps to make sure you are at your best for the sake of yourself and your loved one with dementia. You may need to reach out to family members for support, exploring respite care options, or simply allowing yourself the grace to rest. Caregiving truly takes a village.

The Burnout Spectrum

A visual infographic, "The Burnout Spectrum," illustrates burnout's progression from early signs to full manifestation. It highlights key symptoms at each stage, offering a visual roadmap for caregivers to identify where they might be on this spectrum.

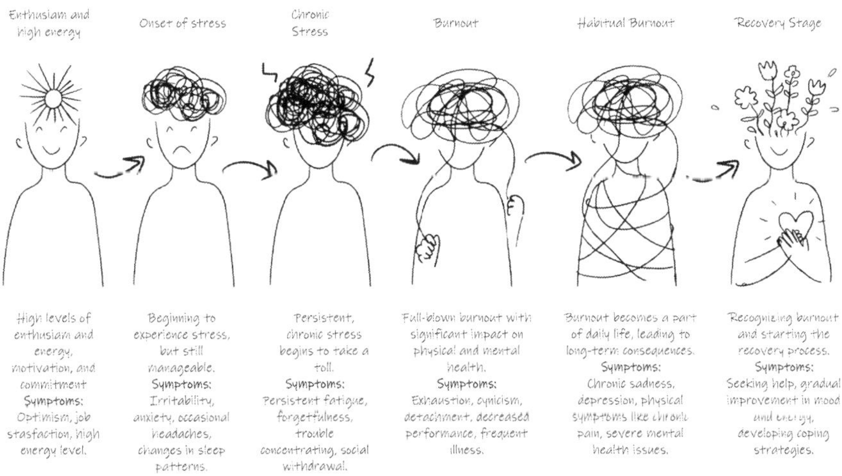

Figure 2: The Burnout Spectrum

A visual guide such as this can be instrumental in helping you recognize the signs of burnout. Once you identify that the way you are feeling is burnout, you can start on the path to self-care.

13.2 The Importance of Physical Health and Exercise

One of the best ways to combat caregiver burnout is to boost your personal well-being through exercise and proper nutrition. It's not a luxury, but a necessity. When you focus on your health, you improve your mood, your immune system, your heart health, your fitness level, and your disposition.

Exercise Benefits

Physical activity has benefits for both body and mind. When you get your heart pumping and your muscles moving, you grow stronger and build endurance Beyond the tangible benefits to physical health - lowered blood pressure, enhanced flexibility, reduced risk of chronic disease - exercise releases endorphins which clears the fog away from your brain, improves your mood, and gives you renewed energy.

Practical Tips for Incorporating Exercise

Integrating exercise into a caregiver's schedule demands creativity and flexibility, an acknowledgment that even brief spurts of activity can have a positive impact. Recognize opportunities throughout your day: a brisk walk in the morning, stretching as the coffee brews, dancing to a favorite song. These actions accumulate. For those tethered closely to their loved one's side, exercise can even be a shared experience. Go for a short walk or enjoy some gentle yoga with your loved one.

Nutritional Needs

Amidst the demands of caregiving, healthy eating habits sometimes fall by the wayside. Yet, your body can't perform at its best if it isn't fed the best fuel. Some days are so hectic that you don't have time to prepare a healthy dinner. Optimal nutrition for the caregiver like you focuses on the simple and accessible. Nutritional meals don't always demand hours of preparation. Fresh fruits and vegetables, whole grains, and lean proteins can take the form of easy-to-prepare sandwiches, salads, and veggie plates.

Sleep Hygiene Practices

Most Americans do not get the recommended amount of sleep on a nightly basis and, for many caregivers, this can be an ongoing issue. Peng, Lorenz and Chang (2019) reported that "poor sleep quality was found in 91.7% of the caregiver participants" in their study.

The key to getting a restful night's sleep is establishing a nighttime routine. A well-followed routine will trigger your brain to naturally release melatonin, allowing you to slowly unwind from the stresses of the day and prepare for rejuvenating sleep. Good sleep hygiene practices also include creating an environment conducive to sleep. Your bedroom should be a haven of tranquility. Remove electronic devices, like televisions and cellphones, from your bedroom and from your nighttime ritual. Studies show that the blue light of electronic devices disrupt our natural sleep patterns.

Creating a Stress-Relief Plan

Caregiving for a loved one with dementia can be stressful. Crafting a plan for stress relief, then, becomes an act of self-preservation during your caregiving journey. To be most effective, your stress-relief plan should be tailored to your own personal preferences. These can include physical activity, journaling, meditation, yoga, or listening to soothing music.

Prioritizing Your Health

As a caregiver, the act of prioritizing your own health is an acknowledgment of their important role in the care of another. To be the best version of you you can be, commit to regular health check-ups, listen to your body, fuel your body with nutritious food. This prioritization is not an act of selfishness. By maintaining your own health, you can continue to provide the compassionate, attentive care your loved ones deserve.

13.3 Emotional Resilience: Coping Mechanisms for Caregivers

Being a caregiver means putting your heart in the line of fire and accepting a bombardment of emotions. This emotional landscape includes grief at the loss of shared memories, anxiety over future uncertainties, or the sharp sting of isolation. This act of naming is the first step toward reclaiming power over these swirling emotions. It allows caregivers like you to see their feelings for what they are so they can develop coping strategies.

Be in the Present

Through the use of coping strategies, caregivers like you can anchor themselves in the present. It teaches the art of observing thoughts and emotions without judgment, acknowledging their presence but not allowing them to overwhelm. This practice can have a calming effect. Mindfulness, in its essence, is the cultivation of a deliberate awareness of the here and now. For caregivers like you, this practice can ground you, steady your emotions, and ease your anxiety. Like mindfulness, meditating may seem frivolous amidst the demands of caregiving, but this is a proven method for calming your emotions.

Journaling

Journaling, too, is an effective coping strategy. The simple act of putting your thoughts to paper can help you sort through your emotions and diffuse their power. Whether in the form of daily reflections, letters never meant to be sent, or creative expression, journaling offers a release, a way to pour out your inner tumult and find tranquility in return.

Seeking Professional Help

Working with a professional therapist can be helpful for caregivers like you. When you meet with a counselor or therapist, you are in a space of unconditional acceptance, where the complex feelings of caregiving can be explored without fear of judgment. Therapists are skilled in navigating the human psyche, and they can offer strategies tailored to you to show you how to deal with current stressors while building resilience for future challenges.

Pursue Joy

Caregivers like you can practice cultivating joy as a tool for reducing stress and increasing your emotional resilience. The pursuit of joy is a concept that may seem cliche, distant, frivolous, or unattainable, especially in the throes of caregiving, but it's an effective strategy strengthening emotional resilience. Joy is often found in the smallest of moments – a shared laugh, the warmth of the sun, a melody that stirs the heart – yet we rarely take the time to appreciate them as they are happening. It requires intention, a conscious choice to seek out and savor these moments, to weave them into the fabric of daily life. Gratitude is a close companion of joy. Like cultivating joy, when we focus our attention on all the things we are grateful for instead of dwelling on the negatives, our mindset shifts.

There will be good days and bad days throughout your caregiving journey. Give yourself permission to feel all the emotions that come with caring for a loved one with dementia. When you experience and process these emotions, you are building your emotional resilience. Through mindfulness, journaling, therapy, the pursuit of joy, and the embrace of professional support, caregivers like you can navigate highs and lows of caregiving.

13.4 Finding Time for Yourself: Balancing Caregiving and Personal Life

The demands of caring for a loved one with dementia can sometimes be so overwhelming that caregivers put their own lives on the backburner, albeit temporarily.

You must have heard of the Oxygen Mask Theory that states if you are on a plane that is about to crash, you should secure your oxygen mask before helping anyone else, including children. If you don't, you risk not being able to help anyone at all.

When you are knee-deep in tending to your dementia patient's needs, it seems selfish to think about your own goals. But you have a right to have a personal life that is separate from your role as caregiver to a dementia patient. In fact, you will be happier, healthier, and better able to carry out your caregiving duties if you find a balance between your role as a caregiver and your personal life. This is when the importance of setting boundaries emerges.

Setting Boundaries

Setting boundaries requires you to be firm in your declarations of time and space that are your own. As a caregiver, you are probably not working traditional 8-to-5 shifts tending to your loved one's needs. You are most likely devoting more than 40 hours per week, taking overnight shifts, and caring for your dementia patient on weekends. Perhaps you even live with your loved one with dementia. It becomes difficult to compartmentalize your time as "on duty" or "off duty" when you are still with your patient. First, acknowledge to yourself that you are prioritizing your personal time, then let other caregivers and family members know. Don't feel the need to explain your decision, justify it, or ask permission. You are entitled to your personal time. Moreover, you NEED it.

Time Management Tips

Your quest for personal time may mean you have to juggle your dementia patient's schedule or complete tasks on a different timeline. By utilizing time management tips, you can make the most of your valuable time and still get done everything that needs to get done. Try starting each day with a To-Do list. When you see all your tasks for the day laid out in front of you, you can prioritize them. Plan to tackle the toughest, most time-consuming tasks when you are at your peak energy for the day. For example, if you have more energy first thing in the morning than you do in the afternoon, arrange to do the most daunting tasks at the start of the day. Lastly, seek out pockets of time that might go wasted and use those to complete smaller tasks. Fold laundry while your loved one with dementia is watching their favorite television show or unload the dishwasher while you are waiting for the pan of pasta to boil.

> Alyssa was still in school while helping her mother care for her grandmother. She had to juggle school work along with her caregiving duties. Alyssa would bring her laptop, chargers, and her notebooks with her everywhere, even at the doctor's office. Whenever she could, she had everything to do her school work. It was not ideal, but she had to be creative to find time for herself.

Importance of Leisure Activities

As part of your personal time, pursue leisure activities that you enjoy and find enriching. Read a book, for example, or tend a garden, paint a portrait, refinish a table, go to a baseball game, or take a walk in the woods. Studies have shown that people who prioritize their personal time and devote this time to pursuing their own passions, interests, and hobbies feel less stressed, are happier, and feel more fulfilled. When they are in these pursuits, caregivers like you reconnect with their identity beyond their role, drawing strength and renewal from these engagements.

Seeking Support for Personal Time

It's vital to have the support of family, friends, and professional services in your quest for personal time. Firmly and assertively explain that you are taking personal time and ask family members to step up to fill the caregiver void from time to time. Do not be bullied or gaslit into thinking it's selfish of you to seek time away from your role as caregiver. It most certainly is not.

If you can't count on friends or family to occasionally help with caregiving duties, you may need to seek outside help. Some community groups and dementia organizations have volunteers who can provide respite services to give caregivers a break. Or, you can hire a home healthcare company to come one or two days a week to allow you some time off. Alternatively, you could send your dementia patient to an adult day care center a few times a week. When you are firm in your need for personal time, you will begin to build a network of other caregivers who you can trust to look after your loved one from time to time, when you need a break. Everyone involved will gain a newfound appreciation for all you do as a caregiver and acknowledge that the caregiver, too, requires nurturing.

13.5 Utilizing Respite Care Services

When you need a break, respite care services can help by giving caregivers some time off. You can hire a respite worker from a home care agency or get help from volunteers, friends, and family. Respite care gives caregivers the chance to recharge and take care of themselves, while also providing a change in routine and socialization for their loved one with dementia.

Do Your Due Diligence

Your loved one with dementia is vulnerable, therefore you will want to thoroughly vet the respite workers you use. If you are relying on friends or family to offer respite care, be sure these people are trustworthy, reliable, and able to handle an emergency situation. Perhaps they should visit a few times while you are there so you can show them the ropes while gauging their capabilities. If you are hiring a home care agency or seeking volunteer respite workers from a community organization, find the agency that works best for you. You need to be sensitive to the care recipient's comfort and dignity and an awareness of the logistical and financial impact. Do your research, collect information, and gather recommendations from fellow caregivers and healthcare professionals. Visit the prospective services, whether in-home providers or daycare centers, to assess the environment, observe the staff's interactions with clients, and get a feel for the overall atmosphere. Ask plenty of questions – what are staff qualifications, the ratio of caregivers to clients, and the availability of activities?

Feelings of Guilt

Caregivers like you often find themselves wrestling with guilt when they seek respite help. A powerful emotion, guilt suggests that seeking respite is akin to abandonment. Despite what you may be feeling, you are most certainly not shirking your duties as a caregiver to a loved one with dementia by adding respite care. It's not a lapse in your commitment but a reinforcement of it. By allowing yourself the time to recharge, you are ensuring that you can continue to provide the high-quality, compassionate care your loved ones deserve. Overcoming this guilt requires an internal dialogue of affirmation, a conscious acknowledgment of the immense value of their work and the necessity of self-care in sustaining it.

As the chapter draws to a close, remember that respite care plays a pivotal role in the caregiving landscape. No one expects you to do everything yourself. This is why there are respite care agencies and services. It's a way you can achieve balance in your life, reconnect with your personal goals, and give yourself some much-needed time away from your caregiving duties to recharge your batteries. Your loved one with dementia will be well cared for in your absence and you will return with renewed energy.

Chapter 14

THE EMOTIONAL SIDE OF CAREGIVING

In many ways dementia is a cruel disease. It robs people of one of their most precious things ... their memories. For the patient, this is as frightening as it's heartbreaking. For the caregiver, it's profoundly sad. In caring for a loved one with dementia, it's natural to find yourself grieving the loss of your family member even while he or she is still alive. The progression of the disease robs the patient of his or her personality, past experiences, and relationships with others. Caregivers get a front row seat to this poignant reality. Not only will you need to reassure your loved one during moments of confusion and distress, but you will have to grapple with your own feelings of loss, sorrow, and the unfairness of fate. The journey of caring for a loved one with dementia is an emotional one for all involved. Anticipate these emotions. Acknowledge them and allow yourself to experience them. But also employ coping strategies and build a support system to help you as you embark on a roller coaster of emotions.

14.1 Coping as a Caregiver

Caring for a parent reverses the normal family dynamic. Our parents are supposed to be the ones who guide us, comfort us, and keep us safe. Dementia upends this. This role reversal can be emotionally trying, especially for caregivers. Ultimately, our goal as caregivers is to make day-to-day life manageable for the dementia patient. It's important to recognize that caregiving is a noble act, but it requires you to balance the needs of the person with dementia with your own.

Caregivers often experience a mix of guilt and frustration. These emotions are a natural response to the challenges and pressures of caregiving. By acknowledging the validity of these feelings, you can find a way to manage your emotions. A study by Losada-Baltar, et al (2024), showed "a significant association between ambivalent feelings and increased depressive symptoms in caregivers over the study period. Similarly, feelings of guilt are found to exacerbate depressive symptoms longitudinally. These findings suggest that both ambivalence and guilt contribute to the deterioration of mental health in dementia family caregivers."

It's easy to forget about yourself while taking care of someone else, but it's important to remember that you need to focus on yourself first before you can take care of others. This means developing self-compassion, recognizing your limits, taking breaks, and continuing to do the things that bring you joy. Give yourself permission to feel happy and sad without judgment.

Remember to accept your emotions and acknowledge the emotions that other family members and caregivers are feeling, even if they differ from your own. By adopting coping strategies to help you with the waves of emotions that come with caregiving, you will be a better, more patient caregiver.

Olivia took care of her husband and stayed overnight at the hospital with him while he was admitted. They do not have any children. Their friends brought food when they visited. On the fourth day, her best friend Emma asked if she needed anything from home. Olivia ended up crying and sharing with Emma that she had been rotating between the three t-shirts she had, washing and drying them in the hospital bathroom. "I have not washed my hair in four days. I feel vain talking about this while my husband is sick in bed."

14.2 The Power of Empathy, Love, and Patience in Caregiving

Understanding the importance of empathy over sympathy is key for caregivers to build strong, meaningful bonds with those they care for. By empathizing and truly experiencing the emotions of the person being cared for, caregivers can cultivate closer and more supportive relationships with their patients.

Developing empathy as a caregiver is crucial in supporting people with dementia. Active listening, paying attention to subtle cues, and imagining oneself in the shoes of the person with dementia are all important aspects of cultivating empathy. This perspective helps caregivers become more compassionate and responsive in their role.

When you develop empathy for your loved one battling dementia, you can use this to frame communication in a way that acknowledges the person's current reality and validates their feelings without dismissing or correcting them. It can be extremely frustrating to find meaning in disjointed or out-of-context words, listen to the same stories over and over again, and understand why the patient is exhibiting a certain emotion or behavior, especially if it seems unwarranted. This approach values effort over accuracy, understanding over correction, and connection over all else.

Caregivers need to adjust their communication methods to meet the evolving needs and abilities of the person with dementia. Put into practice, this means you will need to assess what works and what doesn't, abandon approaches that no longer serve, and explore new methods of engagement. Perhaps using visual aids or relying more on non-verbal cues is now the best way to communicate. Expect to make adjustments to maintain a line of communication that respects the person's dignity and meets them where they are.

Non-verbal communication is also important. Never underestimate the power of a gentle touch, a warm smile, or a supportive nod. Gestures and facial expressions can convey volumes when words fail. Even your tone of voice can convey empathy, patience, and understanding. When caring for your loved one with dementia, be mindful of not only what you say, but how you say it, the look on your face, your posture and mannerism, and how often and how gently you touch your patient.

Empathy transforms the caregiving experience from a dreaded, heartbreaking, and frustrating necessity to an act of love, patience, and a profound sense of shared humanity. Empathy is grounded in active listening, perspective-taking, and adaptive communication as a tactic that not only enhances the quality of care but also enriches the lives of both the caregiver and the person with dementia. The journey of dementia care does not have to be all about the ravages of the condition; it can be about the enduring strength of the human spirit, in the face of adversity.

14.3 Emotional Support Resources for Caregivers

As a caregiver, it's easy to feel like you are going through it alone. That is not the case. There are programs and resources available that provide practical and emotional support for those caring for loved ones with dementia. Your healthcare provider can give you insights into local resources and networks. Hospitals, community centers, libraries, councils on aging, and online community boards are all great places to find resources and support group advertisements. By taking the first step and attending a meeting, you can connect with other caregivers who are going through the same challenges as you. They can offer insight, ideas, new perspectives, and emotional support. As with anything, the more willing you are to become involved in a caregivers support group, the more you will get out of the experience.

Support Groups

The role of a caregiver to a loved one with dementia is as unique as it's demanding. Other people in your life may not truly understand everything you have to deal with on a day-to-day basis. They may offer a sympathetic ear now and then, but can they empathize with your situation? Only other caregivers can appreciate the highs and lows you deal with. Seek out other caregivers ... these are your people. Support groups offer a sense of community and mutual support. Note that you may be able to find specialty support groups, such as groups for Spanish speakers, and for male caregivers. You should be able to find support group by contacting:

- Your local hospital
- Your local council on aging
- Churches and other agencies might host a support groups for dementia caregivers
- Volunteer organizations
- Libraries and community bulletin boards can also serve as treasure troves of information on upcoming events, workshops, and group meetings specifically tailored for caregivers

Benefits of Participation

The act of sharing your story, of laying bare the struggles and triumphs of caregiving, can be transformative, especially when others can validate your experiences. The benefits of participating in support groups extend beyond the cathartic release of pent-up emotions. These groups can:

- Foster a sense of belonging, of being understood without the need for lengthy explanations
- Offer strategies for managing stress

- Provide tips for navigating healthcare systems
- Show you the importance of balancing the demands of caregiving with personal well-being
- Reduce isolation

Online Communities

Online communities, including specialized Facebook groups, are available anytime and anywhere. These resources aim to help caregivers focus on their own needs and provide guidance for moving forward. The Internet is a valuable tool for accessing information and support, with organizations and foundations dedicated to dementia research offering the latest data and forums for caregivers. Social media platforms also host numerous groups and pages where caregivers can exchange tips, articles, and personal stories. It's important to exercise discernment and engage in communities that foster positive and constructive support when utilizing online resources.

> *Dana felt like she was going at it alone while caring for her grandfather with dementia. None of her friends understood what she was dealing with, nor could they offer her any advice. Except her friend, Kim. Kim suggested Dana join the dementia support group that meets at her church every Wednesday night. Dana later told Kim, "I sat in the parking lot until the last possible moment, then I had to force myself to walk in. I planned to just sit in the back and listen, but the people were really welcoming. Before I knew it, I was sharing my story. People nodded in understanding and shared similar stories. For the first time, I didn't feel alone."*

Professional Counseling

Caregiving is physically and mentally taxing. You may experience a range of intense emotions, such as grief, guilt, stress, and burnout that you find hard to deal with. This is normal. Seeking professional counseling can provide a safe and confidential space for you to express your emotions and receive the guidance and support you need. A counselor can help you develop personalized coping strategies, enhance your emotional resilience, and create a non-judgmental environment for healing and growth. Taking the first step can be challenging, but know that you have options. You can consult with healthcare providers for recommendations or explore local mental health services that specialize in caregiver support. Don't wait until your emotional state is in shreds. Get established with a counselor early in your caregiving journey so you can avoid the pitfalls that often come with the job of caring for a loved one with dementia. Remember, you deserve support and care too.

Caregivers are often overwhelmed with the demands of dementia caregiving. Emotional support resources can provide them with the boost they need. These resources come in various forms, such as support groups, online communities, and counseling. Caregivers can seek guidance from these sources and learn from the shared experiences of others. Caregiving may seem isolating at times, but if you seek out support and connect with others who are also caring for loved ones with dementia, things become less isolating and more hopeful.

As this chapter comes to a close, it's important to remember that being a caregiver to a loved one with dementia includes navigating the emotions that come with the initial diagnosis – denial, grief, confusion, and overwhelmingness. Once you, along with other family members, accept the fact that the future will not look how you imagined it would, you can take steps to be more flexible and adaptable. This chapter also touches on the many resources available to help caregivers and the importance of finding your people – other caregivers with whom you can share your questions, fears, and experiences. Seeking connection, understanding, and guidance is crucial as you navigate the challenges and successes of caring for a loved one with dementia. By acknowledging your need for support, you open yourself up to the strength of community, the insights of professionals, and the comfort of shared experiences. This enables you to approach each day with renewed energy and compassion. It's crucial to remember that, in the realm of caregiving, you are never truly alone.

14.4 Navigating Grief and Loss

Understanding Grief in Dementia

Caregivers can grieve for their loved one while he or she is still alive. In fact, this is common among family members caring for dementia patients. It's called anticipatory grief, a mourning for the person's former self, even as they sit before us. It challenges our understanding of loss and forces us to come to terms with a future without the essence of our loved one. Caregivers witness the fading of personality, memories, and abilities, leaving only a semblance of the person they once knew.

John and Eleanor were high school sweethearts who married right after graduation. They spent a lifetime together as husband and wife, best friends, and devoted companions. When Eleanor was diagnosed with dementia, John committed himself to caring for his bride of sixty years as the disease progressed. On the day of their 60th anniversary – after they had enjoyed a nice meal John prepared – the couple moved to their porch to enjoy the beautiful evening. John began reminiscing about the day he proposed to Eleanor. He recalled out loud how he got down on one knee and said, "Eleanor, my belle-amour, will you marry me?" Then he noticed a look of confusion cross his wife's face. "Who is Eleanor?" she asked. John explained, "That's the moment it really hit me that the person I love was fading away right before my eyes."

Stages of Grief

Psychologists have outlined a series of stages of grief the average person goes through when experiencing a loss. Grief in dementia care, however, is not a linear process with distinct stages. The feelings of denial, anger, bargaining, depression, and acceptance can happen out of sequence. There is no 'right' way to mourn. Caregivers may cycle through the stages with different intensities and understanding as they experience unique losses and acceptance.

Coping Mechanisms

Dealing with the complex emotions that come with dementia can be challenging for caregivers. Coping mechanisms are essential in helping you navigate this difficult journey. Coping mechanisms can take many forms. For example, support groups, whether in person or online, are a safe haven where people can share their experiences, connect with others who are going through the same challenges, and find insight from others. Support groups show people can see that they are not alone.

Journaling is another effective coping mechanism. Writing down thoughts, fears, and memories can be a powerful way to process emotions and release the weight of grief. Many people find that journaling gives them clarity and solace.

Supporting Each Other

Family members and friends of the dementia patient form a caregiving team. Each member of this team is going through his or her own series of emotions that may or may not align with yours. They may also have their own ideas on what the care should look like. For the sake of the dementia patient, it's important to anticipate differences of opinion within the support system and to have plans in place to address and resolve conflicts. Instead of bickering with others on your loved one's support team, realize that this is a time to pull together and for collective mourning. The act of supporting each other becomes a lifeline, a means of weathering the storm together. Small things like sharing a meal, talking over the phone, or lending an ear can be a source of light in the midst of grief that can alleviate the stress and burden of being a caregiver.

Organizing a memory-sharing evening, where individuals share stories and photos of a loved one with dementia, not only serves as a celebration of their life but also offers a therapeutic outlet for grief. These gatherings allow for a mixture of laughter and tears, and the weight of the loss is shared, lessening the burden for all those who participate.

14.5 Reflective Exercise: Mapping the Landscape of Your Grief

Journaling Prompt

Take a moment to reflect on your own journey through grief in the context of dementia care. On a blank page, draw a winding path, representing your journey through the stages of grief. Along this path, place markers - symbols or words - that signify key moments of realization, pain, acceptance, or support. Reflect on what each marker represents, considering the following questions:

- At what points did you feel most alone, and how did you find your way back?
- Which moments of support stand out, and who was by your side?
- How has your understanding of grief and loss evolved since the onset of your loved one's dementia?

This personal reflection can remind us of our inner resilience, the support we have around us, and the shared humanity that connects us in times of grief and loss. It's important to remember that we are not alone and that we have the strength to overcome difficult times.

Chapter 15

THE FINAL STAGES OF DEMENTIA

Sadly, dementia progresses over time until the patient eventually succumbs to the disease. Patients in late-stage dementia require continuous care and treatment that includes symptom management and, as a caregiver, your role shifts to preserving your loved one's dignity and comfort.

15.1 Disease Trajectory

Dementia, in its late stages, is a whole different animal when compared to its earlier counterparts. Now, your loved one may face significant health complications, ranging from the loss of mobility to difficulty swallowing, each carrying its own set of care needs. Depending on your loved one's condition, you will have to adjust care strategies. This might look like bringing in hospice care, enhancing the safety features in the home, or exploring specialized feeding techniques to address nutritional challenges.

Symptom Management

As your loved one reaches the late stages of dementia, your goal will be to manage their symptoms to make them as comfortable as possible. This may involve a mix of medical treatment with palliative care principles, focusing on alleviating pain and enhancing quality of life. For instance, you could start using soft, adaptive clothing that makes it easier to dress your loved one with limited mobility, develop a system for reading non-verbal cues and interpreting signs of discomfort or distress.

Communication with Healthcare Providers

Maintaining open lines of communication with healthcare providers is crucial during this time. You may find yourself in frequent consultation with a multidisciplinary team, discussing the changes in your loved one's needs and the best strategies for addressing them. This might involve regular meetings to review care plans, discuss symptom management, and adjust medications.

Preparing for Intensive Care Needs

As dementia progresses, your loved one may need around-the-clock care. To take the burden off yourself, you will need to consider additional support options, such as in-home health aides or specialized dementia care facilities. Making such decisions requires careful consideration. You will need to balance your loved one's care needs with available financial resources and family wishes.

Textual Element: Checklist for Late-Stage Dementia Care

- Assess home environment for safety and adaptability
- Explore specialized feeding techniques for nutritional support
- Identify non-verbal cues indicating pain or discomfort
- Maintain open communication with healthcare providers
- Consider options for around-the-clock care
- Review legal and healthcare directives to ensure alignment with care preferences

This checklist serves as a guide for caregivers like you, providing a structured approach to the complexities of late-stage dementia care. It encourages proactive planning and informed decision-making, ensuring that caregivers are prepared to meet the challenges of this stage with compassion and understanding.

In navigating late-stage dementia, you will be called upon to exhibit a level of empathy and resilience that goes above and beyond ordinary care. More so than ever before, you will become the custodian of your loved one's dignity, advocate for their comfort, and interpreter of their unspoken needs. This period is emotional, but it's also a reminder of the nature of life, the enduring power of love, and the profound impact of compassionate care.

15.2 End-of-Life Care: Preferences and Planning

The late stages of dementia mean that the inevitable is fast approaching. There are many decisions to be made during this end-of-life stage and it's best to make them before you and your family are in crisis mode. Advanced care planning will ensure that your loved one's wishes and directives are followed during this final chapter.

Ideally, you and your family have already created and documented your loved one's advanced directives, noting their wishes regarding medical interventions, life-sustaining treatments, and the designation of health care proxies. Now is the time to lean on these documents to guide you through the medical decision-making process. When your loved one's wishes have been stated and documented, it ensures that their voice is heard by family members and healthcare professionals alike.

Palliative and hospice care may be necessary as your dementia patient reaches their end of life. The hospice philosophy is rooted in the goal of maintaining comfort and dignity, while alleviating suffering. Palliative care brings together medical, emotional, and spiritual support for the individual and their family members. Hospice care emphasizes quality of life, ensuring that comfort, respect, and love are emphasized for the patient's end of life. Both modalities of care, while distinct, share a commitment to honoring the individual.

Navigating conversations about end-of-life care with your loved one with dementia can be challenging, especially as the disease progresses and their level of cognition declines. It may be equally difficult to have these conversations with family members. It's an emotional time for everyone, therefore conversations need to be sensitive, honest, empathetic, and realistic. Plan to have these conversations in a private setting – as opposed to over a nice dinner at a fancy restaurant – so people can let their emotions show. After all, this is a difficult time for everyone. It's okay for people to express their grief and sadness.

When legal and ethical considerations come into play, you will have powers of attorney for health care, ensuring that a trusted individual can advocate for your loved one with dementia when they no longer can. As end-of-life approaches, the advance care planning, the provision of palliative and hospice care, and legal documents your loved one puts into place will relieve you and your family from the burden of making quick decisions during an emotionally taxing time. Your loved one's wishes and preferences will have been documented, guiding caregivers and healthcare professionals in the final moments of your loved one's life.

15.3 The Emotional Journey of Letting Go

No matter how expected it is, the death of a loved one is alway a time of profound sadness. As your loved one's caregiver in the final months or years of their life, you probably grew closer to them and cultivated a deep love and admiration for them. It's natural for you to grieve their passing. Processing grief and loss does not adhere to a prescribed timeline or a set of expected stages. Take all the time you need to work through your grief and allow yourself to feel the emotions swirling in you. As your loved one's caregiver, you may mourn the loss of your caregiving duties and your role as caregiver, along with the loss of your loved one.

Taking an active role in funeral planning, burial or cremation arrangements, and organizing a celebration of life event will allow you the opportunity to process your grief while still taking care of your loved final wishes. In fact, funerary rituals – in cultures around the world – are intended to help the living honor the dead, remember their legacy, and prepare themselves to continue living despite their loss. We could say that funerals, viewings, wakes, and celebrations of life are architecture of letting go – public, structured mourning events.

During this time of overwhelming sadness, it's okay to lean on your support networks. Talk to your family and friends, stay in contact with your caregiver support group, talk to your counselor or therapist. You may also consider joining bereavement groups. Share stories and memories with others. Even laugh at the memories you share. Spending time with people, as opposed to mourning alone, will help you find comfort during this difficult time.

You may feel a surge of other emotions during this time period. You may feel relieved that your loved one's suffering is over and relieved that your caregiving days are over. And you may feel guilty because you feel relieved. It's not uncommon for caregivers to feel a sense of relief, like a burden has been lifted off them. It has, after all! Experiencing waves of relief does not make you a bad person or mean that you aren't sad about your loved one's death. Many caregivers feel the same way. Remember, the time you spend as a caregiver was often difficult, stressful, and challenging. It's perfectly normal to have mixed emotions during this phase.

Death is, unfortunately, an inevitable part of the human adventure. Grief and loss, self-compassion and forgiveness, rituals and remembrance, support networks and shared journeys – each element contributes to the emotional side of caregiving. You can take comfort in knowing that your loved one's concluding chapter was one filled with love and compassion.

15.4 Legacy and Memory: Honoring the Life of Your Loved One

Your loved one with dementia likely lived a full, rich life before the devastation of their disease descended upon them. Honor that rich life, and the memories and legacy that have left behind. There are many ways to do this, as we will see. The way in which you honor your loved one's legacy can be as elaborate and detailed or simple and poignant as you want it to be.

Creating a Legacy Project

A legacy project is a way to document and preserve your loved one's life in such a way that it can be referenced and enjoyed by generations to come. It could include creating a memory book or video detailing their life's journey. You can include classic family stories, childhood memories, important milestones, notable achievements, and anecdotes that illustrate their beliefs, values, and passions. Families might gather photographs, letters, and mementos that, when assembled, reveals the rich panorama of the loved one's life. Videos can include your loved one's favorite music, audio narration, and photographs.

The Importance of Storytelling

Storytelling is an ancient art etched into the DNA of humanity that was created to give people a way to share memories and information from one generation to the next. Stories also have therapeutic power for both the narrator and the audience. In the context of dementia care, storytelling becomes a vessel for shared memories, a space where joy, sorrow, love, and loss find expression. Telling the stories of a loved one, whether in intimate family settings or larger community gatherings, is a tool for helping us process our sadness and reflect on the life of the loved one. As caregivers this narrative process is an opportunity for reflection, a re-examination of the caregiving journey through the lens of compassion and understanding. Remind yourself how much you have learned and grown during your time as a caregiver for your loved one with dementia.

Memorializing and Celebrating Life

Honoring the life of a loved one can take many forms. This is a good thing as it lets you and your family select a method that best befits your loved one. For example, if your loved one enjoyed volunteering as a referee for youth soccer games in your community, you could host a tournament in their honor or dedicate a set of bleachers bearing your loved one's name. If your loved one was an avid gardener, you could design and plant a butterfly garden to honor them. You could initiate a scholarship in their memory, plant a tree to honor them, or donate to their favorite charity. Your loved one would be pleased to know that their legacy will be used to help others in their community.

Preserving Memories for Future Generations

At family gatherings, events, and holidays in the future, take a moment to remember the loved one who has passed. Display their photograph or set out photo albums and scrapbooks for others to look at. Teaching children about the loved one, sharing stories, and passing down artifacts with special significance. Seek out ways to carry your loved one's presence into the next generation. Is your niece getting married soon? Perhaps she will want to carry a bouquet of roses from your loved one's garden. Did a grandson make the varsity football team at his high school? He may love to have your loved one's old letterman jacket. When you cultivate a sense of continuity, you are helping family traditions to take root.

15.5 Finding Closure: Coping with Loss and Grief

In the wake of your loved one's death, caregivers like you may find themselves adrift. Navigating this grieving process does not mean being stoic. The best way to find closure is to experience the raw, unvarnished truth of your emotions. Return to your self-care practices during this time and prioritize your well being. Eat healthy meals, get a good night's sleep, exercise, meditate, journal, spend time in nature, and seek help when you need it. There is no quick and easy way to move on from the loss of a loved one. The best you can do is to take one day at a time.

With your caregiving journey over, you have the opportunity to forge a new path. Perhaps you so enjoyed your caregiving experience that you want to look for work as a home care aid or seek employment at a long-term care facility. Maybe your daily journaling exercises unlocked a strong desire to be a writer. Did you enjoy interacting with people at some of the organizations? You may have found your calling as a social worker. Or, maybe you put your job as a teacher, accountant, restaurant manager, or secretary on hold while you took on the role of caregiver. Now is the time to return to your former profession. Reconnecting with friends, family, and the broader community becomes an essential step in finding closure and finding purpose after your caregiving journey is over.

Alternatively, you could choose to advocate and raise awareness. Consider working to change laws, write policies, plan fundraisers, and secure donations for dementia research. You could also raise awareness through social media campaigns and community events.

If you're interested in giving back to your community through volunteer work, consider getting involved in dementia care. There are various ways to help, from working directly with affected individuals to supporting fundraising events and ensuring the smooth operation of care organizations. Volunteering not only benefits others but also provides a sense of purpose and connection with others in the dementia community. It's a chance to contribute to a greater cause and expand your knowledge while making a meaningful impact.

In the aftermath of caregiving, you will find that you are a changed person. As a caregiver to a loved one with dementia, you get a front row seat to the devastation of this disease and how its victims struggle to maintain their dignity and humanity amid the loss of their memories and cognitive functions. You can't watch that happen and be unmoved by the resilience of the human spirit. This transformation will undoubtedly make you more compassionate, altruistic, and caring. In closing, finding closure, navigating the grieving process, emphasizing self-care, reconnecting with others, and embracing new beginnings will aid you as you cope with loss and grief. Even though your caregiving journey is over, you will always carry the memory of your loved one and your time with them as you pursue other opportunities. Your time as a caregiver was marked by highs and lows ... overwhelming frustration and stress, as well as a profound sense of love and compassion. Although the journey ends in loss, it also gives you new-found perspective, skills, and joy.

CONCLUSION

As we reach the conclusion of our journey together through the pages of this guide, it's essential to reflect on the path we have traversed. From the initial steps of understanding the nature of dementia to the complexities of navigating the healthcare system, each chapter has been a stepping stone towards a deeper appreciation of what it means to be a caregiver to a loved one with dementia. We have delved into practical strategies for daily care, underscored the paramount importance of caregiver well-being, and highlighted the dual focus that caregiving demands – attending to both the individual with dementia and the caregiver.

This book has been crafted with the intention of serving as a comprehensive guide, where each section builds upon the last to create a foundation of knowledge, compassion, and resilience. We have explored the symptoms, discussed how to manage them, and emphasized the significance of maintaining the caregiver's health. It's this balance between caring for your loved one and preserving your own well-being that forms the heart of our shared journey.

The power of informed, compassionate caregiving, the necessity of self-care, and the strength found in community and shared experiences are all key takeaways from our time together. Despite the inherent challenges of dementia caregiving, there is an underlying message of hope and empowerment. With the right resources, support, and knowledge, you can navigate this role with confidence, ensuring both you and your loved one find moments of joy and connection amidst the trials.

I encourage you to reach out and build a supportive network, drawing on support groups, online communities, and local resources. The journey of caregiving is made easier because we have others to share the path. Moreover, I urge you to advocate for dementia awareness in your communities. Your voice can amplify the call for greater support, research, and understanding, making a tangible difference in how society approaches dementia care.

As the field of dementia care evolves, I also encourage you to remain a lifelong learner, open to new research, strategies, and perspectives that can enhance your caregiving approach. The landscape of dementia care is ever-changing, and staying informed will empower you to adapt and thrive in your caregiving role.

From the depths of my heart, I express my gratitude to you, the reader, for your dedication and willingness to embark on this learning journey. My time spent working in nursing homes and skilled nursing facilities has shown me the profound impact that informed, compassionate caregiving can have on the lives of individuals with dementia and their families. Your commitment to understanding and supporting your loved one is a testament to the strength of the human spirit.

This book was conceived as a guide, a source of information, and a companion for you in the caregiving journey. My hope is that it serves you well, offering guidance, support, and inspiration whenever you need it. Remember, you are not alone on this path. Together, through knowledge, compassion, and shared experiences, we can navigate the challenges and rewards of caring for someone with dementia. Thank you for allowing me to be a part of your journey.

Affirmations

FOR CAREGIVERS OF INDIVIDUALS WITH DEMENTIA

Caring for someone with dementia is a journey filled with both challenges and profound moments of connection. In the midst of providing care, it's essential to nurture your own well-being and recognize the immense value of your efforts. These affirmations are crafted to empower and uplift you, offering strength, patience, and compassion. Embrace these positive statements as daily reminders of your resilience and the difference you make in the lives of those you care for. Let them serve as a source of comfort and inspiration, reinforcing that you are not alone and your dedication is deeply appreciated.

1. I am patient and strong.
2. I am doing my best, and that is enough.
3. My love and care make a difference every day.
4. My compassion is my strength.
5. I handle challenges with grace and calm.
6. I prioritize my well-being to better care for others.
7. My efforts are valued and appreciated.
8. I find joy in small victories.
9. I am gentle with myself on difficult days.
10. I honor my feelings and allow myself to rest.
11. I am making a difference in someone's life.
12. I embrace patience and understanding.
13. I give myself permission to ask for help.
14. I trust in my abilities as a caregiver.
15. I focus on the present and cherish the now.
16. I am a beacon of love and care.
17. I nurture myself to better nurture others.
18. I recognize my own worth and the value of my care.
19. I am capable of overcoming any challenge.
20. I take pride in the love and care I give.

REFERENCES

Adelman, R. D., Tmanova, L. L., Delgado, D., Dion, S., & Lachs, M. S. (2014). Caregiver burden: A clinical review. *Journal of the American Medical Association, 311*(10), 1052-1060.

Advance Directive for Dementia. (n.d.). *Advance directive for dementia.* https://dementia-directive.org/

Allen, R. S., Hilgeman, M. M., Ege, M. A., Shuster, J. L., & Burgio, L. D. (2008). Legacy intervention family enactment (LIFE) trial: Translating psychosocial interventions for use in hospice. *Journal of Palliative Medicine, 11*(3), 400-408.

Alzheimer's Association. (n.d.). *Home.* *https://www.alzint.org/*

Alzheimer's Society. (n.d.). *Home.* https://www.alzheimers.org.uk/

Bakker, T. J. E. M., Duivenvoorden, H. J., van der Lee, J., Olde Rikkert, M. G. M., & Beekman, A. T. F. (2022). New life transition of former caregivers: Positive mental health and quality of life. *Aging & Mental Health, 26*(6), 1107-1115.

Ballard, C., Gauthier, S., Corbett, A., Brayne, C., Aarsland, D., & Jones, E. (2011). Clinical features and multidisciplinary approaches to dementia care. *The Journal of Clinical Psychiatry, 72*(5), 682-689.

Bastawrous, M. (2013). Caregiver burden—A critical discussion. *International Journal of Nursing Studies, 50*(3), 431-441.

Better Health Channel. (n.d.). *Dementia - Communication.* Victorian Government. https://www.betterhealth.vic.gov.au/health/conditionsandtreatments/dementia-communication

Betton, V., Ebner-Priemer, U., Brunner, M., Zepf, F. D., & Bode, L. (2022). Development of best practice guidance on online peer support and online counselling for young people. *BMC Psychiatry, 22,* Article 275.

Caregiver Action Network. (n.d.). *BIPOC & minority dementia caregiving.* https://www.caregiveraction.org/bipoc-minority-dementia/

Cheng, S. T. (2013). Dementia caregiver burden: A research update and critical analysis. *Current Psychiatry Reports, 15*(7), 352.

Cleveland Clinic. (n.d.). *Caregiver burnout: What it is, symptoms & prevention.* https://my.clevelandclinic.org/health/diseases/9225-caregiver-burnout

DailyCaring. (2018, October 29). *Innovative eating utensils for Alzheimer's: Make mealtime easier.* https://dailycaring.com/innovative-eating-utensils-for-alzheimers/

Gao, L., Lee, J., & Kim, H. (2022). Impact of social support on the health of older adults: A scoping review. *BMC Public Health, 22*, Article 1291.

Groot, C., Hooghiemstra, A. M., Raijmakers, P. G. H. M., van Berckel, B. N. M., Scheltens, P., Scherder, E. J. A., & van der Flier, W. M. (2016). The effect of physical activity on cognitive function in patients with dementia: A meta-analysis of randomized control trials. *Ageing Research Reviews, 25*, 13-23.

HopeHealth. (2020, November 19). *Grieving before a death: Anticipatory grief and dementia caregivers.* https://www.hopehealthco.org/blog/grieving-before-a-death-anticipatory-grief-and-dementia-caregivers/

Losada-Baltar, A., Mausbach, B. T., Romero-Moreno, R., Jiménez-Gonzalo, L., Huertas-Domingo, C., Fernandes-Pires, J. A., Barrera-Caballero, S., Gallego-Alberto, L., Martín-María, N., Olazarán, J., & Márquez-González, M. (2024). Longitudinal effects of ambivalent and guilt feelings on dementia family caregivers' depressive symptoms. *Journal of the American Geriatrics Society, 72*(5), 1431-1441.

Mayo Clinic. (n.d.). *Caregiver stress: Tips for taking care of yourself.* https://www.mayoclinic.org/healthy-lifestyle/stress-management/in-depth/caregiver-stress/art-20044784

Medical News Today. (2024). *How is dementia diagnosed? Tests, criteria, and how to cope.* Retrieved from https://www.medicalnewstoday.com/articles/how-is-dementia-diagnosed

Mental Health Commission of Canada. (n.d.). *Delaying cognitive decline: 6 stimulating activities for people with dementia.* https://mentalhealthcommission.ca/blog-posts/54175-delaying-cognitive-decline-6-stimulating-activities-for-people-with-dementia/

National Health Service (NHS). (n.d.). *How to make your home dementia friendly.* https://www.nhs.uk/conditions/dementia/living-with-dementia/home-environment/

National Institute on Aging. (n.d.). *Alzheimer's caregiving.* https://www.nia.nih.gov/health/alzheimers-caregiving

National Institutes of Health. (2017, September 25). *Studies show benefits of caregiver support programs.* https://www.nih.gov/news-events/nih-research-matters/studies-show-benefits-caregiver-support-programs

Pacific Neuroscience Institute. (2023, February 7). *The unexpected benefits of music therapy for dementia patients according to a geriatrician.* https://www.pacificneuroscienceinstitute.org/blog/dementia/the-unexpected-benefits-of-music-therapy-for-dementia-patients-according-to-a-geriatrician/

Peng, H.L., Lorenz, R. A., & Chang, Y.P. (2019). *Factors associated with sleep in family caregivers of individuals with dementia.* Perspectives in Psychiatric Care, 55(1), 95-102.

U.S. Department of Health and Human Services. (n.d.). *Tips for caregivers.* https://www.alzheimers.gov/life-with-dementia/tips-caregivers

Yale Medicine. (2023). *Lecanemab, the new Alzheimer's treatment.* https://www.yalemedicine.org/news/lecanemab-leqembi-new-alzheimers-drug

The Good Care Group. (n.d.). *What is assistive dementia technology and how it can help?.* https://www.thegoodcaregroup.com/live-in-care/dementia-care/assistive-technology-for-dementia/

Made in the USA
Columbia, SC
12 May 2025

57809064R00083